I0709412

3 WOMEN VOICES PLAYS

TOM PARKS

PARK PLACE PUBLICATIONS
PACIFIC GROVE, CALIFORNIA

Published by
PARK PLACE PUBLICATIONS
591 Lighthouse Avenue #10
Pacific Grove CA 93950
www.parkplacepublications.com

For information and/or permission to produce these plays
contact Tom Parks: mrtobypal@comcast.net

First Edition Published 2015

ISBN PRINT 978-1-935530-56-5
ISBN E-BOOK 978-1-935530-96-1

Cover image: Kyle Ferdinand
Book design and format Patricia Hamilton
Author Photo: William Strom

Printed in the USA

FOREWORD

Stage portraits of the three celebrated and accomplished women in this collection have been attempted many times with mixed reviews from critics and audiences.

There are volumes of biographies, critical commentaries and personal histories of Dorothy Parker, Gertrude Stein, and Zelda Fitzgerald. Clearly, there is no lack of material on which to build engaging depictions of the women who appear in these plays. Their stories resonate today as vividly as ever. We want to know about them and writers want to write about them.

I had the good fortune of seeing Marty Martin's "Gertrude Stein, Gertrude Stein, Gertrude Stein" with Pat Carroll when the show toured the country in the eighties. There have been several films featuring the character of Miss Stein, none of which matches the admirable writing and performance of the Martin play in my opinion.

Mrs. Parker, portrayed by the superb actress Jane Connell, had a short Off Broadway run in 1985. Critics were underwhelmed at the writing but generally delighted with the performer. The film, "Mrs. Parker and the Vicious Circle," was released in 1994 to mixed reviews due mostly to a puzzling performance by the leading lady.

One of America's greatest playwrights, none other than Tennessee Williams, attempted a biographical play about the star-crossed Scott and Zelda Fitzgerald.

"Clothes For a Summer Hotel" opened and closed with mostly negative reviews on Broadway in 1979.

In these three plays I have for the most part let the characters speak for themselves—to tell their stories. Two of the plays are essentially monologues; one is a two character play. For dramatic purposes, especially in "Zelda," I have invented scenes to illustrate and clarify the fragility of the character.

And so, in this collection, here is yet another 'take' on these three graces. I have had the pleasure of spending a great deal of time with them. In one case, I came with some prejudice, which disappeared early on to be replaced with respect and real fondness.

I like these women, these voices. I hope the reader will, too.

Tom Parks

THE PLAYS

WHAT FRESH HELL IS THIS? 1

THE WIT AND WISDOM OF DOROTHY PARKER

SAVE ME THE WALTZ 51

ZELDA FITZGERALD

PARIS IS PARIS IS PARIS 95

GERTRUDE STEIN IN PARIS

What fresh hell is this?

the wit & wisdom of

DOROTHY PARKER

a new play by

TOM PARKS

DOROTHY PARKER (1893-1967) is today considered by many the very reason for the existence of the famous Algonquin Round Table. She was a writer and poet and critic, best known for her gloomy, ironic quips on life, love, death and—marriage, she managed three of them. Dorothy Parker's writing has remarkable literary staying power, greater than many of her American peers. From her first published work she has been in print for over 100 years.

This play is set in a college lecture hall during the early sixties. She's feeling the pinch on her pocket book, necessitating a return to the lecture circuit along with a stint now and then at teaching American Literature to indifferent young adult students at less than prestigious (in her words) "insane asylums."

Mrs. Parker may have a jaundiced eye but if we look carefully we're bound to discover a playful wink or two.

WHAT FRESH HELL IS THIS?
THE WIT AND WISDOM OF
DOROTHY PARKER

***THE SCENE:** A UNIVERSITY LECTURE HALL. BARE STAGE. A LECTERN SITS CENTER LEFT; CHAIR, CENTER RIGHT. THERE IS A CARAFE OF WATER WITH A DRINKING GLASS PLACED ON SIDE OF THE LECTERN, ALONG WITH A SMALL CLOCK AND A PACK OF CAMEL CIGARETTES.*

***SOUND:** THREE BELLS X THREE X THREE.*

***LIGHTS:** AT THE CONCLUSION OF THE LAST SET OF BELLS THE HOUSE LIGHTS DIM AT THE SAME TIME AS THE STAGE LIGHTS COME UP.*

OFFSTAGE ANNOUNCEMENT

On behalf of Hazelton College, the English Department and the American Literature branch of that department, we welcome students and their guests to the opening of the 1964 Spring Semester.

This is a special day for all of us. And a rare treat. We are about to meet one of the icons of American Letters, a writer, social observer, poet, screenwriter, critic, political activist, and wit.

It is a distinct honor to welcome the lady who, at the Algonquin Hotel, would have sat at the head of the table had it not been round. Dorothy Parker.

DOROTHY PARKER ENTERS (STAGE RIGHT). SHE IS 71 YEARS OLD. HER HAIR, NOW GRAYING IS STYLED IN THE FAMILIAR BOB CUT. HER FIGURE IS STILL SLIM; SHE MOVES WITH EASE, IF SLOWLY. SHE WEARS A SMART COSTUME AND IS WELL GROOMED. SHE IS CARRYING A LARGE SCRAP BOOK, HER PURSE, AND A SMALL STACK OF 3X5 QUESTION CARDS. HER VOICE IS MODULATED, SOFT, AND SOMEWHAT SING-SONG. SHE SPEAKS SLOWLY AND WITH PRECISE DICTION, EASTERN SEABOARD, CIRCA 1920.

MRS. PARKER MOVES DIRECTLY TO THE LECTERN, NOT ACKNOWLEDGING THE APPLAUSE FROM THE AUDIENCE. SHE CHECKS THE TIME ON THE CLOCK, SEARCHES FOR HER GLASSES, AND PLACES THE QUESTION CARDS TO ONE SIDE. SHE REACHES FOR THE CARAFE AND POURS HERSELF A GLASS OF WATER, WHICH SHE DRINKS DOWN. SHE TAKES ANOTHER SIP, FROWNS, LOOKING FOR THE FIRST TIME AT HER AUDIENCE.

MRS. PARKER

In the old days that would have been gin. If I'd been Christ at the Last Supper I'd have opted for gin instead of wine. Well, we all have our own tastes.

I thank that nice young man for his words of introduction. I generally don't cotton to all the purple prose used today when we speak of special people, celebrities, rock and roll bands ... icons. History hasn't been very kind to writers but then writers haven't been very kind to history.

I'm here because I was invited. One has to be invited these days. I can't remember even one invitation I received to any gathering; I just showed up. Oh, I loved parties, not for the people, but for the food and drink—or was it the other way around? Besides, I was making ten dollars a week at *Vogue*. Salary was no object, I wanted only enough to keep my body and soul apart. I wrote photo captions for fashion layouts. And speaking of layouts, there were countless debutantes who would vie for the chance to appear in *Vogue*. They were all a-flutter, those girls. The 'coming out' orgy. Darlings, if all those sweet young things were laid end to end, I wouldn't be surprised.

But I'm getting ahead of myself. I've decided to start from the beginning, my beginning, since my end is rapidly growing on me. I don't often do this—these talks. I'm not sure I know what to tell you or what you may want to hear. Strangely, there's been much written about me over the years. Now, I don't care what's written about me so long as it's not true. Writing is a miserable profession, if it can be called a profession. Now, I suppose I shouldn't say that. I'll try to think of something positive about writing so I can get us through this in plenty of time for a double Old Fashioned before Mass.

This large tome I've hauled up here is what used to be referred to as a scrapbook. You know, with the soft, ecru papers, where one artistically placed photos with specially designed, glued corners of grandma and her fourth husband whom we refused to call grandpa. And brother, Clarence, still with his baby teeth at thirty three.

No, that's not what this is—well, not really. It's my filing cabinet, you see. I'm a terrible organizer and lose things all the time. Besides I've lived in so many places—rooming houses, apartments, hotels of various reputations—and no real possessions such as the sofa, the leather chair, the smoking stand, the cockatoo? So this file goes everywhere I go—it has its own passport.

More importantly, it holds my notes to myself, pictures of past pals, some scribbled verse. And a kind of biography of who I am and where I've been. I can answer the latter question far better than the former.

SHE OPENS THE SCRAPBOOK, TURNING A FEW PAGES AT RANDOM.

My God, here I am at three with my father. His name was Rothschild, a Jew. My mother was Irish Catholic. As I can recall I wasn't knocked out about either one of them. I hated my name—not Dorothy, but Rothschild. Why do you think so. My guess is that the parents weren't crazy about it either. It was the times—Jews were not what you'd call society's darlings. My mother left me, well, she died, when I was five. The old man remarried soon thereafter. Too soon? Probably. He found himself a new wife, a former school teacher. Now, she was a piece of work—very religious.

Can you just imagine coming in from school, where you were taught nothing, and finding this creature greeting you at the door with, "Did you learn to love Jesus today?" Jesus!

I taught myself to read and I read everything. I read Dickens, Thackeray, Stevenson, Twain—even the Greeks. And I certainly learned something from the Greeks!

Goodbye to all that, I say. (Or someone did.) I entered the great city of New York—by the way, did I mention I was born in New Jersey? By that standard even Cleveland wouldn't have been bad. Hung out in a rooming house with a collection of women who were searching for careers … or husbands. Certainly not both.

Then, by some miracle I became Mrs. Parker. I wonder if I married him so I could change my name. Nice chap. Gone so fast I didn't have time to change the bed linen. The war, you know. Lest we forget: "the war to end all wars." Not something I coined, I assure you. Here and gone was the husband. *(CHECKS HER BOOK)* Here's a rather good photo of him—comely. Did I write this? Not bad. "Husbands. And whenever you go out to have a good time, you always meet them."

Now it was time to get serious. Time to pay the rent, to buy a little nothing frock, time to boil the cabbage for dinner. Found myself a job at *Vogue* in an office the size of a bottom drawer.

Fashion stuff. But I just couldn't take those endless yards of fabric seriously. I acted up … or down some would say. The editor moved me to *Vanity Fair*, far more to my liking. A swell magazine. And it was there that I met my lifelong chum, Mr. Benchley, Robert Benchley. We had the same sensibilities, the same humor and the same jaundiced eye. He was in the modern world but not of it. Everything serious had to be challenged and he did it with irony, wit. Now, there's my kind of man. We palled around together daily. We hit every speakeasy, every open (and closed) house to mooch Ritz crackers and bad gin and worse conversation. Now, I don't want to suggest that we were … we weren't. Mr. Benchley was a happily married man with the kids to prove it. We were best friends.

What to do? We shared a tiny office, the size of two bottom drawers, atop Carnegie Hall. We met every day for lunch, and for evenings that seemed to go on until the rooster does … whatever a rooster does. I was still at *Vanity Fair*. Office hours were not for me even though by this time I was making twelve dollars a week—a sizable salary in those days. In my spare time I wrote what I called my 'hate poems.'

REFERRING TO THE SCRAPBOOK

It's in here somewhere, the one I want to read—here it is.

OUR OFFICE

I HATE THE OFFICE,
IT CUTS INTO MY SOCIAL LIFE
THERE IS THE BOSS;
THE GREAT WHITE CHIEF.
HE MADE US WHAT WE ARE TODAY—
I HOPE HE'S SATISFIED.
HE HAS SOME BIZARRE IDEAS
ABOUT HIS EMPLOYEES GETTING TO WORK
AT ABOUT NINE O'CLOCK IN THE MORNING—
AS IF THEY WERE A LOT OF MILKMEN.
HE HAS NEVER BEEN KNOWN TO SEE YOU
WHEN YOU ARRIVE AT 8:45,
BUT TRY TO COME IN AT A QUARTER PAST TEN
AND HE WILL ALWAYS GO UP
IN THE ELEVATOR WITH YOU

Now, I suppose that sounds a little bit sour. Well, I did say it was one of my "hate poems." And I wrote a lot of those.

My editor—the chap in the elevator—began to assign me as a vacation replacement for the drama and literary critics. Ah, just my cup of hemlock. I have to say I lasted only as long as the two holiday-makers were out of town. Seems as though I was a tad tough on what I saw and read.

Here are some of my 'considerations' of past theatre seasons.

IN THE FIRST ACT THE HEROINE IS STRANGLED BY ONE OF HER ADMIRERS. FOR ME, THE MURDER CAME TOO LATE.

Here's another about a Broadway hit:

THE SCENE IS LAID IN FRANCE, THUS GIVING EACH MEMBER OF THE CAST A CHANCE TO PRONOUNCE THE WORD 'MONSIEUR' IN A DIFFERENT WAY. BUT THEN, AS THE OPTIMISTIC WOMAN JUST A LITTLE WAY IN FRONT OF ME OBSERVED, "WELL, IT'S A CLEAN SHOW, ANYWAY."

I find this quite invigorating:

CHANNING POLLOCK'S NEW PLAY IS CALLED "THE HOUSE BEAUTIFUL." WELL, "THE HOUSE BEAUTIFUL" IS THE PLAY AWFUL.

I had a few thoughts on actors:

THE EVER LOVELY MARION DAVIES HAD TWO EXPRESSIONS: JOY AND INDIGESTION.

... And on actresses. Katharine Hepburn in the new play, "The Lake":

MISS HEPBURN RUNS THE GAMUT
OF EMOTIONS FROM A TO B.

X DOWNSTAGE: TO LADY IN FRONT ROW

I'll wager you've heard that one before.

About actresses in general:

HER NAME, CUT CLEAR UPON THIS
MARBLE CROSS,
SHINES, AS IT SHONE WHEN SHE WAS
STILL ON EARTH;
WHILE TENDERLY THE MILD
AGREEABLE MOSS
OBSCURES THE FIGURES
OF HER DATE OF BIRTH.

Surely you didn't for a moment think I would quote one of my positive reviews? What fun could that be?

For *The New Yorker* I wrote as 'The Constant Reader.' I reviewed the new books on the Strand. Seems the magazine took a lot of flack from its readers on my account. I must have given offence. I can't for a moment imagine why.

MR. A.A. MILNE, HE OF THE NEW OFFERING, *THE HOUSE AT POOH CORNER*, HAS HIS CHARACTER, PIGLET, ASK POOH WHY HE HAS ADDED THE PHRASE 'TIDDELY-POM' TO A SONG, AND POOH ANSWERS, "TO MAKE IT MORE HUMMY."
AND IT IS THAT WORD, 'HUMMY,' MY DARLINGS, THAT MARKS THE FIRST PLACE IN *THE HOUSE*

AT POOH CORNER AT WHICH TONSTANT
WEADER FROWED UP.

Poor A.A. Apparently I couldn't leave the chap alone.

For my swansong in the critic's corner I contributed a last hurrah entitled, *When We Were Very Sore.*

DOTTY HAD
GREAT BIG VISIONS OF
QUIETUDE
DOTTY SAW AN
AD, AND IT
LEFT HER
FLAT.
DOTTY HAD A
GREAT BIG
SNIFTER OF
CYANIDE.
AND THAT, (SAID DOTTY)
IS THAT.

Well, that *was* that. *Vanity Fair* fired me. I said my goodbyes in a final paragraph:

GOODBYES ARE BEST SAID BRIEFEST. SO I
THANK YOU ALL SO VERY MUCH AND THOUGH
I CERTAINLY HAD A ROTTEN TIME,
I HAVE TO LEAVE YOU.

And that I did—for *The New Yorker.* Kicked upstairs as they say. I was a new person (well, not really). I decided

I needed a change of scene. A new apartment would be right for starters. The handsome real estate agent showed me a flat on West 57th Street—a better neighborhood than I deserved. "Oh dear," I said, "That's much too big. All I need is enough room to lay a hat and a few friends."

Now, you'll want to know about the Algonquin, a hotel that was opened in about 1902 as the Puritan, a temperance hotel. My goodness, it wasn't long before that changed.

Mr. Benchley, Robert Sherwood, and I were on our uppers with very few coins in our purses. Close to our office stood the Algonquin. We learned that the hotel served hors d'oeuvres at lunchtime, gratis. Just our style, a couple of drinks and a scoop of egg salad. This was then our new watering hole. The manager/owner was eager for publicity so he encouraged lit' types to his front door. So we (the lit types) took him up on his offer. In force.

So here you have Robert Benchley, Robert Sherwood, Mrs. Parker, Franklin P. Adams, Alex Wolcott, Haywood Broun, Harold Ross, Harpo Marx, George S. Kaufman, and, now and then, Edna Ferber. A rather driven lady—God knows, certainly not a beauty—but with a considerable wit. Noel Coward joined us one noontime. He stared at Edna and said, "You almost look like a man." She looked him in the eye and replied, "So do you." Edna had her redeeming qualities.

We called ourselves The Board. We were originally gathered in what is now called the Oak Room. Soon thereafter, as our numbers and guests increased, we moved into the Rose Room and sat about a round table.

Ergo, "The Round Table," or as some (certainly not one of us) preferred to call it, "The Vicious Circle."

People romanticize it. The Round Table was no Mermaid Tavern, I promise you. These weren't giants. Think of who was writing in those days—Lardner, Fitzgerald, Faulkner, Hemingway. Those were the real giants. The Round Table was just a lot of people telling jokes and telling each other how good they were. Just a lot of loudmouths showing off, saving their gags for days, waiting for a chance to spring them. It wasn't legendary. I don't mean that, but it wasn't that good. There was no truth in anything they said. At first I was in awe of them because they were being published. But then I came to realize I wasn't hearing anything very stimulating. I remember hearing Wollcott say, "Reading Proust is like lying in somebody else's dirty bath water." Yes, I'd had enough of the Round Table.

Now, I have a feeling you didn't want to hear this said of the myth, the romantic period of American literary expression, and all that. And far be it from me to shatter your fantasies. I'm not saying it wasn't good fun or that the daily gatherings weren't often times witty, clever, silly. And I? Frankly, I was just a little Jewish girl trying to be cute.

But I certainly participated (after a drink or two). I was probably misquoted more than any of 'em. But I, just as the rest of them, was showing off. Damn, it was the twenties and we had to be smarty. I think it was Herman Manckiewicz who said, "The greatest collection of unsaleable wit in America."

With the 'Crash' in '29 came the end of the Round Table. There didn't seem to be anything even mildly amusing to say about the poor souls on the street. The moment had passed. And speaking of passing, so did Ring Lardner and Heywood Broun in '39; Woollcott in '43; Benchley in '45; Ross in '51; Sherwood in '55; FPA in 1960—we're getting close—Kaufman in 1961. My God, and here I am, a person who has more than one time toyed with death, the last of the lot.

FARTHEST AM I FROM PERFECTION'S HEIGHTS,
FAULTY AM I AS I WELL COULD BE,
STILL I INSIST ON MY SHARE OF RIGHTS,
WHEN I AM DEAD, THINK THIS OF ME:
THOUGH I HAVE UTTERED THE WORDS "YEA,
BO."
THOUGH I USE "AIN'T" TO GET A LAUGH,
THOUGH I AM WONT TO EXCLAIM "LET'S GO,"
THOUGH I SAY "YOU DON'T KNOW THE HALF"—
BLACK THOUGH MY RECORD AS DARKEST JET,
GIVE ME, I BEG, MY DEVIL'S DUE,
ONLY REMEMBER I'VE NEVER YET
SAID, "HOW'S THE WORLD BEEN TREATING
YOU?"

A long time ago there was something called 'society.' And that is not a comment on the current usage of the term. After all, we have a certain muddled something called society today if you consider the seriousness of the war in Asia, waste in government, poverty, busing, the bomb. No, I'm speaking of society as in, well, 'society.' And now you're completely confused.

Newspapers from the turn of the century until quite recently devoted unconscionable amount of ink to the going's on in the posh houses in big cities and small towns. The big city was, of course, New York. Still is. Only, God knows, there's not a trace today of the kind of society I'm referring to and that's not a bad thing. But refer to it I will.

It was important, in days long gone, for those in the creative arts to "appear" in society. I, and most of my chums, did just that. We had our reasons, you see. We needed to be seen, known, celebrated, adored, and fed. The moneyed folks on the Upper East Side threw lavish parties and wanted to entertain their equally rich friends. We were sought after. It was a good deal: they got free entertainment by the top literary giants of the day and we got 'saw.' Plenty of booze and tiny sandwiches. Lots of laughs. Let's face it, it was we poor guys doing the slumming. At one of these soirees a hefty matron fell all over herself when she spotted me holding twin scotch and sodas. "Oh my dear, are you really Dorothy Parker?" Yes, do you mind?

Well, they certainly didn't mind. They loved us and we merrily ate and drank our way through countless over-sized, over-done, and over-rated town houses of the over well-healed.

I can't remember even one of those evenings. I don't have to. My biographers and followers seem to remember every flippancy I'm credited with uttering. I suppose one could say the joke's on me, for here I sit quoting myself—or someone quoting herself, quoting me.

Pithy I was called. And I'm not going to comment on that.

Sherwood's wife finally had a baby whose arrival she'd talked about endlessly. I'm supposed to have said, "Dear Mary, we all knew you had it in you." Not bad.

Someone walked up to Dotty (that's me) and asked if I was enjoying the party. "*Enjoying* it? One more drink and I'll be under the host."

Benchley's son swears this is verifiably true. President Coolidge had died.

> Benchley: "Coolidge is dead."
> Parker: *(innocently)* "How could they tell?"
> Benchley: "He had an erection."

And they go on and on and on.

Yet at another terribly amusing party, another terribly amusing remark—apparently I was just full of it.

A friend walks up to Parker to inform her that a mutual lady friend had passed on. "The poor, dear thing," says the friend, "she was a nice person who wouldn't hurt a fly."

Parker: "Not if it was buttoned up."

Now, that's enough (for now). Imagined or real, I cannot keep my face shut.

Now I know you in this hall tonight have your

questions. And here are some of them on the cards you filled out earlier. I've chosen a few to talk about; others I just couldn't bare to read, let alone answer. What has been for me so maddening, at times down right painful, is that if I'm to be remembered, at least for six or seven days after I check out, I'd like to be remembered for something other than the most quoted (and misquoted) ditty I wrote many years ago.

MEN SELDOM MAKE PASSES
AT GIRLS WHO WEAR GLASSES

Therefore I refuse to quote it. I have no desire to disappoint those of you who are unaware of my three or four other writings. Some absolutely devoid of puns, smarty retorts, flash, cynicism, or down right rudeness.

LOOKING OUT OVER HER GLASSES AT THE AUDIENCE

There, you see, I've disappointed.

I was told by management that there surely would be questions from those of you here tonight. It's not that I don't like surprises but I prefer to be prepared for the unknown. I mean, what if someone asked me for housekeeping hints or my shade of lipstick or even with whom I was currently stepping out? (Do people use that phrase today?) But those are the easy ones. And the answer to all is zero. I have here some questions on small three by fives. I'll do my very best.

Here's Donald, who asks, "What is your take on politics?"

Young man, I think it's politics that's been on 'the

take' as long as I can recall. I'm what is referred to as a liberal. Now, there's a modifier to that—goddamn. I've been involved in liberal causes for many years, even when I didn't know I was liberal. It just seemed right to me, or was it left? My heart and soul were with the cause of socialism. The thirties, for instance, were the progressive days. We thought we were going to make the world better—I forget why we thought it, but we did. Roosevelt to us was a God. The missus? What a woman. It's hard to believe, but when you met her, she was the most beautiful woman you ever saw.

I made the train journey to Boston to protest the death sentences for Sacco and Vanzetti. There I was, all five feet of me on the line for justice. When I tell you how mean some of the spectators were, I mean *mean*. At one point the crowd turned in my direction and shouted, "New York nut!" "Red scum!" and "Hang her!" Not for my writing, for which I really couldn't blame them. Well, they didn't hang me but they electrocuted poor Mr. Sacco and poor Mr. Vanzetti.

Anyway, they jailed me and pushed me about in the slammer. I emerged on bail, rumpled and sticky, to be greeted by a rather large contingent of reporters. "How was it, Dotty?" What the hell did they think? My response: "I thought prisoners set free got five dollars and a suit of clothes." That was one of the low points in the thirties.

And yes, I did 'dip my toe' into red waters, but not an entire leg. Many of us admired what Russia was doing for the people. We weren't as smart as we thought we were.

Donald Ogden Stewart, Freddie March, Oscar

Hammerstein and I helped found the Hollywood Anti-Nazi League in '36. That move came back to haunt me twenty years later. I marched with the writers, the studio workers—we, a few of us, invented the American Screenwriters Guild, yet another thorn in the side of the Hollywood bosses. Payday was coming.

As I look back at that period, a period where the word 'union' was a vulgarism; where black people had no voice; where even the right to express an opinion was considered treasonous by some. Acceptance of the status quo is what hurts you in all forms. You get soft and don't stand up on your hind legs. When the day comes when you can accept injustice, anywhere, well, what's the point of living?

Oh, I was relentless in those days. I hired on as a reporter for *New Masses* and went deep into Spain at the start of the Civil War. What I saw was Guernica times ten—the slaughter, the misery. I took the Fascist victory badly, along with other countless Americans who fought with the Loyalists. Oh, by the way, there was another war, '39 to '45.

I played it straight—well, as straight as I could without shutting my mouth. I believed in that war and the men and women who fought it. The Algonk days were long gone. Mr. Benchley and I remained pals as did some of the Round Table residue. We did what we could. Of all my lit pals, only Alan saw the front. Alan Campbell, my second husband, about whom later.

The next thing worse than war is the stuff that

hits the fan. In 1952 Mrs. Parker received a subpoena from the friendly folks of the House Un-American Activities Committee. The FBI had kept a long file on me for several years. References cited all sorts of suspect behavior: 'possible subversive,' 'premature anti-Fascist,' 'Communist leanings,' 'snippy to mother-in-law.' Joe McCarthy was riding high in this low jinks. I appeared. Dressed to the eights, I might add. "Are you now or have you ever been a member of the Communist Party?"

My response: "I was and am many things to myself and to my friends. But I am not a traitor and I will not be involved in this obscene inquisition."

And I added that I didn't even know what a Communist organization was. But the last word is never a last word for me. I stood my ground addressing those piranhas on the bench: "Look, I can't even get my dog to stay down. Do I look to you like someone who could overthrow a government?"

I was blacklisted. And for all intents and purposes, including making a living, I didn't work for five years.

Let me add one last bit of color to the period. My last editor, who will remain nameless because he has all the definable qualities of a bastard, told me if I changed my position on the Spanish Civil War and praised Franco, he would publish me. "God damn it," he said, "why can't you be funny again?"

SHE ONCE AGAIN LOOKS OUT AT THE AUDIENCE

And that, young man, is my take on politics.

EVERY LOVE'S THE LOVE BEFORE
IN A DULLER DRESS.
THAT'S THE MEASURE OF MY LOVE
HERE'S MY BITTERNESS:
WOULD I KNEW A LITTLE MORE,
OR VERY MUCH LESS!

On the subject of love I'm a great authority. Well, that's an understatement. An understatement under a pile of rejection, hope, failure, duplicity, hide and seek, resignation. Everything except recrimination. I'm sorry for none of it. I did marry, thrice. Parker went to war. He must have liked it for I saw very little of him after that. We lived more apart than together, and I'm not saying that's a bad thing. God, aren't all words connected with marriage horrible? Connubial, nuptial, spouse. Is that the best we can do? Actually, I require only three things from a man. He must be handsome, ruthless and stupid.

I've had, in my time, many friends. My lady friend is Lillian Hellman. That's singular. I prefer the company of men, always have—oh, so many of my men pals, Benchley and Charlie MacArthur, Alex Woolcott, Harpo, Alan Campbell (why is it I keep putting him off?), Frank Adams, Bob Sherwood, and a cast of thousands.

Having said that, I have at least one of them to thank for a pregnancy. Why the hell am I thanking him! I had an abortion, yes. That, it seems, is what I got for putting all my eggs in one bastard.

Let me tell you now, I'm not ecstatic about aging. It's a damned nuisance. What I mean is, there are far fewer chances to flirt, to fantasize, well, to nail someone. Age comes with indignity in life's threadbare pageant. I don't like it. People ought to be one of two things, young or dead. What's the good of fooling?

There are ways to get around it; beat it at its own game. Pills, booze, a forty-five. I know, believe me. I was in rehearsal for many years. Thankfully the show closed out of town.

RAZORS PAIN YOU;
RIVERS ARE DAMP;
ACIDS STAIN YOU;
AND DRUGS CAUSE CRAMP.
GUNS AREN'T LAWFUL;
NOOSES GIVE;
GAS SMELLS AWFUL;
YOU MIGHT AS WELL LIVE.

And another:

THERE'S LITTLE IN TAKING OR GIVING,
THERE'S LITTLE IN WATER OR WINE;
THIS LIVING, THIS LIVING, THIS LIVING
WAS NEVER A PROJECT OF MINE.

And another:

IT COSTS ME NEVER A STAB NOR SQUIRM
TO TREAD BY CHANCE UPON A WORM.

"AH, MY LITTLE DEAR," I SAY,
YOUR CLAN WILL PAY ME BACK ONE DAY."

I thought that might cheer you. I'm very good at reading audiences. You see, I have a dark side. With all the witticisms attributed to me one would naturally assume I was a card, a laugh a minute, a funny lady. I like the occasional joke. The only thing is that my jokes tended often to be on the 'noir' side.

I recall many years ago when I found myself in a hospital room after having made a rather elaborate theatrical attempt to knock myself off. (Don't ask me why—I can't possibly remember all of my adventures to leave this planet.) So there I am propped up in bed reading Nietzsche—or was it Jacqueline Susanne—and scarfing down chocolates when Mr. Benchley walks in. He stuttered, paced the floor, coughed, paced, stuttered, coughed. Finally … "Dottie, if you don't stop this sort of thing, you'll make yourself sick."

I developed an early preoccupation in my life to anticipate the end of it. Some people doodle; I've been known to compose—my epitaph. Let's see, there was "Pardon My Dust," "This Is On Me," "If You Can Read This, You Are Standing Too Close." A modicum of wit in those I would think.

I have been known to take an occasional aperitif or ten. Have you ever had what is referred to as a 'hangover?' I have had several of museum quality. Then there are what I call the 'Rams.' Much like the heebie-jeebies except that they last longer, strike deeper, and are, in general, fancier.

Now, I'm convinced that very often these 'Rams' may be directly traced to the mastication of a bad stalk of celery.

Here is the proof of my detective work. I was served celery (my favorite food) at a gathering one evening. That stalk must have been bad because you can't tell me that two or three sidecars, some champagne at dinner and a procession of mixed Benedictine and brandies are going to leave a person in that state where she is afraid to turn around suddenly lest she see a Little Mean Man about eighteen inches tall, wearing a yellow slicker and roller skates.

Besides the continued presence of the Little Mean Man, there are minor symptoms of faulty knee action, heartbreak, an inability to remain either seated or standing, and a constant sound in the ears as of far off temple bells.

These together with a readiness to weep at any minute and a racking horror of being left alone, positively identify the disease as the Rams. Bad celery will give you the Rams quicker than anything else. You want to look out for it. There's a lot of it around. My doctor warned me on one occasion that if I didn't stop drinking, I'd be dead within a month. Promises, promises. Mr. Benchley persuaded me to consult Alcoholics Anonymous. I did go to a meeting and found the whole organization just adorable. Next time I saw Mr. Benchley he asked me if I'd decided to join. I told him in no uncertain terms that I would not. They wanted me to stop drinking … now.

Another card? This is a question from GL. And just

from the handwriting I'll guess that GL is female. Anyway I hope so. "Why did you choose to become a writer? Do you write every day? Where do you find inspiration?" Inspiration mostly comes in the form of a scotch and soda.

I do not write every day. Sometimes I find myself at the typewriter at three in the morning; other times I work in taxis, trains, ships—on and off—work never interfering with my social life. Weeks, months go by when I haven't typed a semi-colon. Then the landlord appears at my door and all at once I have a deadline.

I've inevitably been a person to spend a great deal of time alone. Well, I suppose one could say that of many writers. Most of the time our work—yes, it is work after all and should be considered so—this work spans days and weeks and months of solitude.

I use many excuses not to write and, in that exercise, I can be very creative. Never having been a house person; by that I mean cooking, cleaning, doing whatever must be done to make the little cottage cozy for my man when he returns home from the plant to find a steaming plate of pot roast at his place at the head of the table. No, this is not my style.

I find a cocktail most helpful to begin my aforementioned exercise. Well, perhaps two cocktails depending on the work in progress, the length of the piece and the day of the week. Actually, any day of the week will do, thank you.

I am particularly fond of nail buffing. I can spend hours on my thumbs alone. Then there is rearranging my shoe collection according to season and color. I would not, for instance, ever file a pair of white Mary Jane's next to my black patent leather pumps with the zircon clips—I just wouldn't.

I must confess I am a consummate listener to the daily fifteen minute radio dramas. What Stella Dallas will do with her snobbish daughter, Laurel, and her wicked mother in law; not to mention how she will keep her best friend, Min Grady, and the knit shop afloat means a great deal to me. I can't wait for Monday to roll around to see how the latest crisis has been resolved only to learn there is yet another crises that will carry me through the rest of the week.

So you see, more times than not, writing, the actual putting of words to paper, can be an avocation. The exercises not to write seem infinitely more interesting.

Writing for me does not come easily. I'm not a disciplined person. I'm terribly self-judging and unsure. Acclaim means nothing to me—good reviews do not cheer me. Doubt is my master.

I believe the purpose of the writer is to say what he feels and sees. I began writing in a new feminist world, where there were no longer firm rules to guide women. Rage, loneliness, emptiness—the lot of women. I wrote what I saw, and what I saw was a tragic view of life. No happy ending there. I was one of the lucky ones, I lived the life I wanted (or thought I wanted). At the same time I had to make a living. I hated all rich people but I thought I'd be absolutely adorable with money. I wanted to write but I wanted to be rich too. And, having to make a choice between letters and loot, I'd go for the coin.

From an early age I wrote verse because I couldn't bear the stuff others were scribbling. My verse (I've never been able to call it poetry) was what it was; anyway it didn't do any harm. It didn't roughen my hands or mind, just as you can say of knitting.

And light verse was the style of the day. What I wrote was a bit darker than most. Certainly eons removed from the exquisite poetry of Edna St. Vincent Millay, who was so fashionable and so right for her time.

Ultimately, I've become known as a humorist. This characterization is unpleasing to me. I don't want to be classified as a humorist. I've never read a good, tough, quotable female humorist, and I never was one myself.

I couldn't do it. A 'smart-cracker' they called me and that makes me sick and unhappy. There's a helluva distance between wisecracking and wit. Wit has truth in it. Wisecracking is simply calisthenics with words. Now, satire is something else again. They're the big boys. If I'd been called a satirist, there'd be no living with me.

I would never say I am a woman-writer. That would be, and would have been, the end of any readership I might have found. At the same time, I can't think of a man–writer with the name Dorothy. God knows there's Evelyn and Marion and Connie. So please, if you ever refer to me say, over the butcher counter, explain me away by calling me "the dame who wrote 'men seldom make passes' … oh, never mind.

On a lighter note. That is if you consider the subject of marriage "lighter." At last I come to my second husband,

Alan Campbell. Alan was an actor and a writer—my goodness, what a combination. We were married and we were divorced. And we were married. It was 1934 when we co-joined. The first few hours were bliss. And then I met his mother. Actually, it was the best time in my life—we had a good time. It's that simple, it was fun. I was eleven years older, not what you'd call the child bride.

Speaking of marriage, honeymoons and happiness—in none of which am I an expert—I ran into one of my former publisher's agents in the hallway just now. He reminded me of a telegram I sent him when Alan and I were on the West Coast sleeping in our virginal marriage bed. This was in response to his wire which pleaded for more pages for my forthcoming book. My answer he recalled was, "Too fucking busy … and vice versa."

Over the years I threatened to send Alan to military school. As it turned out, I didn't need to. In '42 he went to war just as Mr. Parker had done twenty five years earlier. But I'm getting ahead of myself, ourselves.

There is a place where fairies live; it's called Hollywood. Mr. Benchley was the first of my pals to head for land of hooey; that was the late twenties. Alan and I followed with the promise of an MGM writing contract. Now, the difference between a writer and a Hollywood writer … in Hollywood the writer comes into his office, takes off his coat, sits at his typewriter, puts the paper in, puts his fingers on the keys and waits for the phone to ring. The only-ism Hollywood believes in is plagiarism. I hate movies; they lower my vitality.

I found I had nothing to do. A grand office was

mine. The air was oppressive. I recall one mid-afternoon throwing open the windows and shouting out at some tourists, "Let me out, I'm as sane as you are!"

Nobody can do anything alone in Hollywood. You are given a script that eight people have written from a novel four people have written. Over the years I worked on many scripts for many studios, mostly uncredited—so you see, there really is a God. And everyone there wrote. I never saw such a thing. The nice man at the gates would write. My hairdresser wrote. The producer would write—and that was much worse.

After some weeks, I ran away. But Alan and I returned after marrying. It was then that the producer/genius/manic-oppressive David O. Selznick contracted us to write the screenplay of *A Star is Born.* And we did it with no little success. Nominated for an Academy Award. Lost out to *The Life of Emile Zola.* Never met the man.

One very good experience in Dreamland was working with Lillian Hellman on dialogue for "The Little Foxes." I had by this time exasperated producer Samuel Goldwyn who would tell anyone on the lot, or on the street, for that matter, that he didn't understand a word I said, ever. Now this is the same Samuel Goldwyn famous for his malapropisms, fractured English, and general disconnect from reality. One night my phone rang long past midnight; What fresh hell is this, I wondered? It was Sam Goldwyn.

"I've seen the rushes, and that picture, *The Little Foxes,* is Communistic. It's Communism pure and simple, I tell you."

"But Sam," I said, "the story's set in the early nineteen hundreds. There wasn't any Communism then."

"Thank God!" Then he added, "Dorothy, do you really say all those things the papers report you say?"

"Do you?"

I actually appeared on screen one time. It was in a Hitchcock picture Alan and I worked on for about five minutes, *Saboteur*. Hitchcock had a habit of showing up in all his movies. The scene finds Hitch and Dotty (a couple) sitting in a car observing the leading man slapping about the leading lady. She (me) opines, "Oh, they must be very happy." Catch it sometime.

Alan Campbell and Dorothy Parker divorced in 1947. Dorothy Parker and Alan Campbell married in 1950. Blame it on Hollywood.

You may have been curious about this beautiful collection of cigarettes. Cigarettes with no ashtray, although in the past I've been known to flip an ash here and there. No, these lovely packages are there to remind me that I can resume smoking anytime I like. I've done quite well in my abstinence *(CHECKING THE CLOCK)*— it's been about fifty-two and a half minutes as I read it.

BACK TO THE SCRAPBOOK

Here's a photo of Edna, that's Edna, as in Ferber. And another of Kaufman with Ferber. I wasn't very kind to poor, homely Edna. But then she was making so much money from those pot-boiler novels she didn't give a damn. I never really related to Kaufman even though we collaborated now and then. And Alex Wolcott—

he owned an island off the East Coast. Lillian and Mr. Benchley and I, and too many others, spent weekends with Alex on his 'spread.'

I think it must have been Bob Sherwood who, very impressed with the extensive forest surrounding the main house, enthused over the variety of flora. "Beautiful, Alex," he said, "This is obviously why you bought this paradise—for the trees."

"Nonsense, there wasn't a green branch here when I moved in."

"You mean you *planted* this forest!"

Alex looked over the treetops and explained: "I planted this forest because I figured that's exactly what God would have done given the same opportunity." Unusual for Woolcott to give credit to anyone, not the least of whom was God.

When I speak of the past, the past somehow manages to seem present. All those years of chumming with good friends. The loves, the hates, the silly arguments, the hurt feelings, the bruised alliances. And the lovely times of too much love and open affection, undiminished loyalty—they all seem real and ever present. Not many of them around today, fifty years later.

I think of Gerald and Sara Murphy in Cap d'Antibes. They called their house Villa America and I think that the whole of America must have stopped there. I had on and off again moments with Gerald but Sara was always ready for me. I was particularly fond of their children. Hemingway was very good company if a bit high on himself—well, he was our greatest writer at the time. He was often with the Murphys. As was Cole Porter and Linda, Picasso, Charlie Mac Arthur—this is the early twenties. Too much sun; too much booze; too much ego. But as the Murphys taught us, "Living well is the best revenge."

When I look back, and these days I can't help but look back, I'm astonished at the people I knew, the creative geniuses/failed geniuses/geniuses in disguise/geniuses with no genius. Hemingway, Fitzgerald, Hellman, Levant, Edmund Wilson, Marc Connelly, Bennett Cerf, The Barrymores, Fannie Brice, Chaplin, Gershwin, Larry Hart, Janet Flanner, Maugham ... sometimes I think I must sound like a smug name dropper. Ah, but what names I could drop. I was touched by some of them and ran like hell from others. Darlings, if we had more time, I'd like nothing more than to reveal something just awful about all of them.

Men seldom make passes ... well, I'm not going to say it. What I am saying is that my quips, the dismissive witticisms, critical judgments—have, over the years, pegged me a complete misanthrope. And I began believing just that.

However, reexamining my work, it seems I have a rather sentimental bent. Nothing cloying, mind you. In fact, in these verses from various times in my life, I apparently just couldn't leave love and romance alone to soar. No, there always seems to be a twist here and there. I wonder why? Well, I don't wonder why at all.

This is called *Day Dreams.*

WE'D BUILD A LITTLE BUNGALOW,
IF YOU AND I WERE ONE.
AND CAREFULLY WE'D PLAN IT, SO
WE'D GET THE MORNING SUN.
I'D RISE EACH DAY AT ROSY DAWN
AND BUSTLE GAILY DOWN;
IN EVENING'S COOL YOU SPRAY THE LAWN
WHEN YOU CAME BACK FROM TOWN.

A LITTLE COOK BOOK I SHOULD BUY,
YOUR DISHES I'D PREPARE;
AND THOUGH THEY CAME OUT
BLACK AND DRY,
I KNOW YOU WOULDN'T CARE.
HOW VALIANTLY I'D STRIVE TO LEARN,
ASSURED YOU'D NOT COMPLAIN!
AND IF MY FINGER I SHOULD BURN,
YOU'D KISS AWAY THE PAIN.

I'D BUY A LITTLE SCRUBBING-BRUSH
AND BEAUTIFY THE FLOORS;
I'D WARBLE GAILY AS A THRUSH
ABOUT MY LITTLE CHORES.
BUT THOUGH I'D COOK AND SEW AND SCRUB,
A HIGHER LIFE I'D FIND;
I'D JOIN A LITTLE WOMEN'S CLUB
AND CULTIVATE MY MIND.

IF YOU AND I WERE ONE, MY DEAR,
A MODEL LIFE WE'D LEAD.
WE'D TRAVEL ON FROM YEAR TO YEAR,
AT NO INCREASE IN SPEED.
AH, CLEAR TO ME THE VISION OF
THE THINGS THAT WE SHOULD DO!
AND SO I THINK IT BEST, MY LOVE,
TO STRING ALONG WITH YOU.

This next rhapsodic piece is titled, *Song of the Open Country.*

WHEN LIGHTS ARE LOW, AND THE DAY HAS DIED,
I SIT AND DREAM OF THE COUNTRYSIDE
WHERE SKY MEETS THE EARTH AT THE MEADOW'S END
I DREAM OF A CLEAN AND WINDSWEPT SPACE
WHERE EACH TALL TREE IS A STANCH OLD FRIEND,
AND EACH FRAIL BUD TURNS A TRUSTING FACE.
A PURLING BROOK, WITH EACH PURL A PRAY'R,
TO THE BENDING GRASS ITS SECRET TELLS;
WHILE SOFTLY BORNE ON THE SCENTED AIR,
COMES THE FAR OFF CHIME OF CHAPEL BELLS.
A TINY COTTAGE I SEEM TO SEE,
IN ITS QUAINT OLD GARDEN SET APART;
AND A SABBATH CALM STEALS OVER ME,

WHILE PEACE DWELLS DEEP IN MY BROODING
HEART.

AND I THANK WHATEVER GODS LOOK DOWN
THAT I'M LIVING RIGHT HERE IN TOWN.

I warned you there are a few twists? I just can't help it.

OH, LIFE IS A GLORIOUS CYCLE OF SONG,
A MEDLEY OF EXTEMPORANEITY.
AND LOVE IS A THING
THAT CAN NEVER GO WRONG—
AND I AM MARIE OF ROMANIA.

In 1934 I wrote the lyrics to a song with music by Ralph Rainger. And, upon my soul, I can't find one twist in the whole damned thing. It's called *I Wished on the Moon.*

EV'RY NIGHT WAS LONG AND GLOOMY,
SHADOWS GATHERED IN THE AIR.
NO ONE LISTENED TO ME,
NO ONE WONDERED DID I CARE,
NONE IN ALL THE WORLD TO LOVE ME,
NONE TO COUNT THE STARS THAT HUNG.
THEN THE MOON CAME OUT ABOVE ME
AND I SAW THAT IT WAS YOUNG.
I WISHED ON THE MOON
FOR SOMETHING I NEVER KNEW,
WISHED ON THE MOON
FOR MORE THAN I EVER KNEW.

A SWEETER ROSE,
A SOFTER SKY,
AN APRIL DAY
THAT WOULD NOT DANCE AWAY.
I BEGGED OF A STAR
TO THROW ME A BEAM OR TWO,
WISHED ON A STAR
AND ASKED FOR A DREAM OR TWO.
I LOOKED FOR EVERY LOVELINESS,
IT ALL CAME TRUE.
I WISHED ON THE MOON FOR YOU.

I will not sing that song tonight.

SHE CHOOSES ANOTHER QUESTION CARD

JC asks..—now, promise me that's not Jesus Christ—I'm not up to Him this evening.

So JC asks, "Mrs. Parker, what do you think of the literary scene today—what are you currently reading?" First things first. There have always been bad writers; some just bad, others more badder. But maybe worse than bad writers are the bad publishers. I mean by that that publishers have become ink pimps. Editors, if such animals exist at all today, are the madams, and the readers are the tricks. (And the metaphor, along with God, is dead.)

Anything that even suggests s-e-x is published and is sold. Tell-all books that take us into the bathrooms of so called celebrities are ghosted by men and women who should have been flushed down at birth. And the countless biographies of Hollywood's mechanical dolls are a torture to read, but then so is *Moby Dick.*

Fiction writing hasn't changed much and there's more of it than ever. There has however been an interesting turnabout. In the old days New York writers were lured to movie fantasy land. Today it's the Hollywood writers who are clamoring to the mean streets of New York. And that's why we can be grateful for the likes of the Messrs. Irving Wallace Harold Robbins, et al. These gentlemen never saw a vagina or penis they didn't like. It is, therefore, cause for celebration that their offerings remain on the best seller lists for weeks on end.

And since you asked me what I am currently reading, JC, I will tell you. I have quite recently discovered that there is a kitchen in my small rental pied a terre. The agent was proud to announce that it was fully equipped. That, I assumed, meant that there was a stove in the kitchen. Since I had never before put my head into an oven (if I'd only known) or even stood before one, I called Saks and ordered an apron. This is perhaps more than you want to know, JC. The direct answer to your question—what I am currently reading is *The Complete Better Homes and Gardens Bread Cookbook.* I have yet to try my luck. The recipe calls for an egg. Saks doesn't carry eggs.

On East 74th Street, just off Central Park there was and is a wonderful resident hotel called the Volney. When I last left Hollywood and returned to New York (kissed the very pavement, I did) I wanted a new beginning. It was 1952 and the old Volney was a grand choice.

Quentin Reynolds was living there also. I told him the Volney was right for me in two ways. First I loved the accommodations and second, it was just next door to Campbell's funeral parlor.

We talked about the serendipity but I said I certainly didn't want to be carted out on a stretcher like any other stiff. He came up with a lovely idea. We should try to convince the management to erect a chute from my floor into the back entrance of Campbell's. I'd arrive in good condition and the trip would take but a minute. Our suggestion was declined; I can't for a moment understand why.

As it turned out the Volney was the inspiration for a play I was about to write. And write it I did. *Ladies of the Corridor* is a play about women without men, living lives on their own—yearning, making do, going about, as TS Eliot said, "measuring their lives in coffee spoons." Not a complete flop, the play had some good and some tepid reviews. I personally gave hell to Brooks Atkinson. But George Nathan named it the best play of the season. It closed after just six weeks. And I have to say today that *Ladies of the Corridor* is the only thing I have ever done in which I had great pride.

1956 brought great expectations. It was the year of collaboration with Leonard Bernstein, Lillian Hellman, Richard Wilbur, James Agee and John Latouche. The show was *Candide*, a musical pastiche based on Voltaire's novel. I had only one lyric in it. The show didn't work out very well. Too many geniuses. We all got along fine except John Latouche who died. The show failed and went dark after 73 performances. The thing was so over-produced that you couldn't tell what was going on at all. It's been revived time and time again, pared down, pumped up but with the same dismal results.

I struggled, paced the floor, cried, took to the razor, and generally beat myself up to write a novel. Ultimately the journey exhausted me. Yes, I was a successful with several collections of verse under my girdle; many short stories which were well received—I never got the reviews I thought I deserved. But the novel. That's what I wanted so desperately to write. My short story, *Big Blonde*, was praised by the people who counted. Could I expand on that? I gave it two or three years with nothing to show my publisher in the end. Maybe I was too close to "Big Blonde"; it was considered by some to be autobiographical. That was not my intent. And yet... Oh, what the hell, maybe it was, is. I could use a drink.

I dislike to disappoint and I haven't very often. I've been called many things from acerbic to rude, to mean, to bitchy. I confess to all the above. If you were kinder than I, and as I look out and view your faces I see that you must be, you might say that I'm "not easy to love." Beats the hell out of "bitchy," wouldn't you agree?

You see, I'm often a stranger to myself. I've met and been in the company of many, but just for a very few did I establish lasting friendships. And even those were at times tested more than once. It has been written by a long time acquaintance that "Dorothy Parker is a combination of Little Nell and Lady Macbeth." I have no argument with that.

I have my good points, honesty being one. I may have used humor in some of my critical writings, much to the abhorrence of the writer or playwright in question, but the point was made—this is bad writing. I was and am a critic and that's what critics do, they criticize. God knows I've had my own work bloodied by more than one established critic. In my case I never forgave them.

In New York I seemed to have known everyone in the arts. And we all thought we were just darling. In Hollywood I knew everyone and liked no one. And I thought I was just darling. In Europe I was the eternal house guest. And that turned out to be good news and bad for my hosts. We formed close ties of affection. But when I moved on it was over.

In New York I lead a rather solitary life, not without some pleasures—well, the New York Times for one. I see some people, my neighbors, the darling lady who does for me and the young man who brings me the new books in large print.

Still all through my life long term friendship has eluded me or vice versa. And to be absolutely honest, I think it's the latter. No complaints, no excuses. I must have planned it this way. "At my birth, the devil touched my tongue."

Alan Campbell died last year. What a strange marriage, and I can multiply that by two. Much younger than I. Handsome, talented to a certain degree. He really convinced me to go to Hollywood for the first time so he could become an actor. We loved and fought. Probably fought more than loved. We both threatened to run away from home more than once. Never did. Never had pocket change enough to buy a bus ticket. The fights were terrible. And looking back it was more than just terrible, for Dotty always won.

How in hell we laughed these episodes off I'll never know, but we did and found ourselves in love again—for the next few days anyway. I was never quite sure of his sexual preferences. I think he must have been straddling the fence. There were times when I thought he was as queer as pink ink. But who knows and who really cares? Look, we all know that heterosexuality is not normal; it's just common. Alan would come and go geographically and emotionally. The latter hurt most. We lived on the wrong side of the tracks in a dreary little bungalow in dusty, over-heated Hollywood. I picked up a job teaching at a minimum security junior college where the student population learned early on to hate me. And to be honest I can't blame 'em. I was miserable living in LA and I longed for the under-heated NYC. One night Alan walked into his bedroom and closed the door. He was finished with life, which with a little help from a few pills finished him.

Lillian Hellman tells this story, and for the life of me I don't remember it at all, not for a minute. It was at Alan's wake in Los Angeles. Someone came up to me, the grieving widow, and asked if she could get me something. I supposedly replied, "Get me another husband." She was horrified and said so. "OK, then get me a ham on rye, hold the mayo." Another quip attributed to Mrs. Parker? Who knows; who cares. The point was, Alan was dead. And I could have used a ham on rye.

It seems I've always been short of money. Banks giveth and banks taketh away. I'm speaking of credit. The two greatest words in the English language are 'cheque' and 'enclosed.' I have been and am constantly overdrawn.

What to do? Well, write, Dotty, write. And that's what I've always done. But early on I learned to sweet talk my publishers with promises of pages to come if only they would advance me a thousand. And those boys did and that's the way I lived. There was one time I recall when I attempted to open a charge at a rather fancy department store and was refused. I complained to anyone who would listen, but it was Alex Wolcott who responded with a fake carbon copy of his reply to the store on my behalf:

"Dorothy Parker has given my name as a reference in an attempt to open an account at your store. I hope that you will extend this credit to her. Surely Dorothy Parker's position in American letters is such as to make shameful the petty refusals which she has encountered at many hotels, restaurants, and department stores. What if you never get paid. Why shouldn't you stand your share of the expense?"

I cannot remember a time when I was not living considerably beyond my means—perhaps I should say beyond the pale. I didn't let it get me down, I just kept spending. I'm older now and God knows what will happen to me. And here's what I think about that: money can't buy health, but I'd settle for a diamond studded wheelchair.

X DOWNSTAGE: TO LADY IN FRONT ROW

Never mind, darling, I have car fare to get me home tonight.

I've never developed a flair for saying goodbye. Oh, I've screamed and cried and thrown things and threatened and cajoled and even swigged shoe polish. (Don't try it;

there are other ways.) But to graciously remove myself from a scene is not my forte. I believe the people whom I meet today—well, here, for instance, in this very hall, they think they know me. At one time in my life I thought I knew who I was, too. You out there may be closer to the truth than I. In fact I'm sure you are.

As the years have passed I'm less sure of who I am. Is this age speaking? No doubt. Is it maudlin or arrogant to wonder how I'll be remembered? No doubt again. Still I do wonder. And we all know I can't do a damned thing about it.

I wrote this some years ago for Robert Benchley.

LIFE COMES A-HURRYING,
OR LIFE LAGS SLOW;
BUT YOU'VE STOPPED WORRYING—
LET IT GO.
SOME CALL IT GLOOMY,
SOME CALL IT JAKE;
THEY'RE VERY LITTLE TO ME—
LET THEM EAT CAKE!
SOME FIND IT FAIR,
SOME THINK IT HOOEY,
MANY PEOPLE CARE;
BUT WE DON'T, DO WE?

And then I wrote this for myself:

FOUR BE THE THINGS I AM WISER TO KNOW:
IDLENESS, SORROW, A FRIEND AND A FOE.
FOUR BE THE THINGS I'D BEEN
BETTER WITHOUT:
LOVE, CURIOSITY, FRECKLES AND DOUBT.
THREE BE THE THINGS I SHALL NEVER ATTAIN:
ENVY, CONTENT, AND SUFFICIENT CHAMPAGNE.
THREE BE THE THINGS I SHALL HAVE TILL I DIE
LAUGHTER AND HOPE AND A SOCK IN THE EYE.

This life can be a long journey, or less than long journey. Mine has seemed brief, so far anyway. I'm blessed with selective memory—what a wonderful gift. I'm blessed also with having had good and fair and loyal pals and who deserved better than what I handed most of them. Happily, they too had selected memories. But the past is the past and each new day needs to be celebrated. Or endured. Whatever talents I possess, whatever I leave behind, is for others to judge, just as I have judged. Let them say what they will. It's a Goddamned law.

I've enjoyed your company tonight even though it was I who did all the talking. I've always felt more secure in a crowd than on my own. I wonder why, I'm told I'm very good company.

SHE TURNS TO EXIT.
RETURNS TO CENTER STAGE

On second thought I do know how I'd like to be remembered. Only three words, quite simple.

Dorothy Parker, writer.

SHE EXITS.

CURTAIN

Zelda
Save Me the Waltz

ZELDA FITZGERALD (1900-1948) was born Zelda Sayer in Montgomery, Alabama. Even before she rose to fame as "America's First Flapper" she managed to become a celebrity in her home town. A prankster, cut-up, artiste, boy-chaser and general nuisance to her family, especially her father, Judge Sayer. Life was swell and with Zelda around life was one long party.

Enter struggling writer F. Scott Fitzgerald who courted and won her. Together they owned New York. Scott published his iconic novel, *The Great Gatsby*, and became known as America's greatest novelist. Gradually, Zelda became erratic and difficult, entering asylum after asylum to bad diagnoses and dangerous medications.

This play is set in an Asheville sanitarium in 1948. Zelda remains connected to life through art and religion. She's forthcoming about her history, the halcyon days and the endless, dark interludes which have haunted her for much of her life. This is a courageous Zelda who has made a bargain with herself—life will go on. For how long will it go on is the question she seems never to ask.

ZELDA
SAVE ME THE WALTZ

A SANITARIUM, ASHEVILLE, NORTH CAROLINA 1948.

A COMFORTABLE SITTING ROOM. TWO FRENCH CHAIRS, A TABLE/DESK CENTER STAGE WITH A PORTABLE TYPEWRITER, A PILE OF PAPERS, GENERAL CLUTTER. UPSTAGE LEFT, AN EASEL WITH A WORK IN PROGRESS. NEXT TO THAT A SMALL TABLE WITH A JAR OF BRUSHES AND A PALETTE OF OIL COLORS.

THE CHARACTERS

ZELDA SAYER FITZGERALD, 48. LOOKS HER AGE, 5'4", GRAYING BROWN HAIR, PLAIN, NO MAKEUP, WEARING A PAINT SPLATTERED SMOCK. SHE HAS BEEN WORKING; HER HANDS HAVE EVIDENCE OF PAINT ON THEM. SHE HAS PROBING EYES, CLEAR, INTELLIGENT. SHE SPEAKS WITH AN EDUCATED SOFT ALABAMA TINGE. SUBTLE, BUT THE SOUTH IS THERE.

HENRY PIPER, 25-30. BRIGHT, SENSITIVE, HOPING FOR A FIRST INTERVIEW FOR NEW CAREER ON THE LOCAL NEWSPAPER.

AS THE CURTAIN RISES WE FIND BOTH ZELDA AND HENRY CENTER STAGE. THEY HAVE JUST MET.

ZELDA

Now, tell me again, please, Mr. Piper, what is the name of your newspaper?

HENRY

It's the *Florence Morning News* out of South Carolina. I'm assigned to the local culture page.

ZELDA

CALLS OFFSTAGE AS SHE MOVES TO COVER THE CANVAS SHE'S BEEN WORKING ON

Charmaine dear, will you please leave the door open just a little for some cross ventilation, it's summer time in the South and we can't have Mr. Piper faint from heat exhaustion now can we.

CHARMAINE

OFFSTAGE

Miz Zelda, you know the rules, I don't make 'em. This door should remain locked at all times, doctor's orders. I just work here.

ZELDA

Honey, I'm well aware of the rules but our guest is not. I'm not going anywhere. This will be between the two of us, Charmaine. (FIRM) Once again, we need some air in this stifling room, leave the door ajar. Please.

CHARMAINE

OFFSTAGE

Aw right, but I'm not gonna take responsibility. I need this job. I'll be right out here in the hallway.

ZELDA

There's a sweetheart. I'll buy you an ice cream soda down Halliday's drug. What flavor?

CHARMAINE

OFFSTAGE

I'll be in the hallway.

ZELDA

BACK TO MR. PIPER

The culture page. Well, this world can certainly use some culture these days. I hope the *Morning News* has more than one culture page.

And you've come here this lovely late afternoon to interview me. That's what you wrote in your sweet little note but, Mr. Piper, what I'm inclined to believe is that you're really here to talk about F. Scott Fitzgerald, especially now that his books are in print again. Why, he's having a kind of renaissance these days. I wonder, is it possible for a dead person to have a renaissance? My goodness, there's new hope for all of us. Those of us who seem to have lived a kind of death for years.

HENRY

CAUTIOUSLY

Yes, ma'am. Well, there couldn't be a story if it didn't include you, Mrs. Fitzgerald. I've read so many ...

ZELDA

Of course you have. Now, we must decide right from the beginning how we will address each other. For instance, I have never been called Mrs. Fitzgerald, although I *was* Mrs. Fitzgerald I was also Miss Sayer and Zelda Sayer. But never "ma'am." You must decide. I have made *my* decision. I'm going to refer to you by the name on your calling card. Mr. Piper. Yes?

HENRY

Yes, that will be fine. May I call you Miz Sayer?

ZELDA

You may even call me Zelda if you like. The New York Times did. But that was a long time ago. I wonder what they'd call me today, assuming they'd call me at all.

Now, Mr. Piper, let me offer you a chair.

INDICATING TABLE/DESK. THEY SETTLE.

I suppose like all young American men you are a baseball fan. So you will understand the metaphor when I tell you that this table is my home base. This is where I read, where I write and where I make my momentous decisions of the day—that is when I am in residence.

And when I am not in residence I am in my hometown of Montgomery, Alabama, where I share a small cottage with my mama and where I entertain my dear lifelong friends, those that haven't left town for fun and riches in the city. And if they have been so fortunate to have found those city riches, they keep in touch with me on the telephone, a wonderful way of communicating.

You know when I first found myself in New York City—I had just married—everybody telephoned everybody, we were always telephoning, telephoning. It was very exciting. It was all about nothing, of course—what we said. Telephoning, telephoning. But it was fun. We all had such fun. Fun was our fare. And that's what I told Scott when our baby was born, Scottie, our daughter. "Scott," I said, "I don't care if this baby is smart or clever, I just want her to have fun. I want her to have fun and be beautiful and rich." I wish I could write a book about worlds and people who live by the gay philosophy of popular songs. Well, as it's turned out our daughter is beautiful, a mother, rich. I don't know if she has fun. Times have changed—well, they always do—I don't think people have the fun we had then. Fun is fleeting, fleeting.

Tell me, Mr. Piper, do you believe in God? Well, of course you do, we all do. Well, heavens, we all *should* believe in Him. Scott was a Catholic but I'm not sure he believed. Catholics are very peculiar people, don't you agree? They call it, their religion, the *Church*—spelled with a capitol 'C' don't you know—the *true* church. Well, I don't know about that. What about the Methodists, Lutherans? Are they not *true*? So much for those Catholics.

Scott and I never attended church except for the occasional funeral. Well, in those years nobody died, we were all so young!

Mr. Piper, you must speak up. Surely you have some questions to ask for the culture page.

Speaking of Montgomery, there simply couldn't have been a more startling difference to a young lady of 19 when she first set foot in the lobby of the Plaza Hotel on Fifth Avenue in New York City. Scott had published several short stories in the popular magazines so he was somewhat known. But I? I was the wife, an unknown quantity. *(LAUGHS)* It didn't take long for that to change.

But first Scott insisted I have a wardrobe which was right for the life we intended to lead in the city. I was all flounces and chintzes but he wanted to see me in the height of New York fashion, sophistication. And that height turned out to be a black Patou costume which I hated. More and more shopping until I just said 'enough' and began inventing my own *sense of fashion*. And I'm delighted to report that my sense of fashion was copied by many an aspiring Flapper. (LAUGHS) Years later in Rome, yes, I think that's where it was, I found that Patou at the bottom of a large steamer trunk. Certainly it was the worse for wear thanks to legions of international moths. Out it went. And I had never once worn it.

I wonder if you're interested in fashion, Mr. Piper?

HENRY

I don't know much about fashion, Miz Sayer. But I know it played a certain role in the 20s, I mean the world of Flappers and, as your husband called it, "The Jazz Age."

ZELDA

The Jazz Age.

HENRY

And if I'm not mistaken, Zelda Fitzgerald was considered the most talked about Flapper of the day.

ZELDA

LAUGHS

You're not mistaken, Mr. Piper. But there were so many of us. The only thing that was expected of a Flapper was to be outrageous. In dress, personality, morals—and for the most part we didn't disappoint. The war had ended, there was money again—let the fun begin.

We hadn't a care in the world, Scott and I, nor had we a dollar in our handbags. Broke most of the time, we spent and spent and spent. We were so very happy, just married, in love. Scott was becoming more and more successful. We thought we had everything. But everything wasn't enough for us. Theatre, nightclubs, dance halls, concerts, cocktail parties, weekends in the country—they weren't enough. It was peculiar, hard to explain today. We always wanted something to *happen*. It wasn't enough for us to show up at a Park Avenue penthouse, we wanted to make mischief and we did. Pranks like falling off balconies, spiking drinks, taking baths fully clothed in the host's tub. Terrible. *And wonderful*. Or at least we thought so. Others were not so sure. Of course we drank too much, inebriated every night. We were evicted from at least three hotels, three or four, with our baggage on the sidewalk. Arrested for disorderly conduct for bathing in the fountain in front of the Plaza; Scott eviscerated our second hand Marmon when he drove over a fireplug. And then there was the night at *The Scandals* when during the second act, Scott took off all his clothes. I fell into the aisle laughing and we were both thrown out of the theatre.

Scott's "Jazz Age" lasted just a few years. Prohibition was almost never enforced if you knew the right politician. The Flapper moved on and the Market flopped, which didn't bother us at all since we didn't have a dime. That was when Scott started borrowing on his advances from Scribner. And he did that for the rest of his life.

What is your favorite book, Mr. Piper? Mine is the Bible.

HENRY

Well, I own a Bible but have to confess I haven't opened it in many years.

ZELDA

Open it now and then, Mr. Piper. You will find it comforting. You look to me like a Baptist. I, myself, am not a churchgoer, but if I had to choose, I might just consider the Baptist persuasion. But the Bible's the thing, forgive the Christian reference to Mr. Shakespeare.

HENRY

You mentioned Scribners. They were your husband's publishers I believe.

ZELDA

They were. It was Harold Ober, his agent at that house, a best friend, and in so many cases a financial savior. Max Perkins edited Scott. They brought him along from his early magazine pieces to his first successful novel in 1920.

HENRY

This Side of Paradise.

ZELDA

This Side of Paradise. It sold over 40,000 copies. A bestseller.

Critics loved it. He was so proud. I was proud for him. You know, Scott had a large ego. Now, that is not always a bad thing, and not necessarily a character flaw. When we first met at a dance in Montgomery—he was a lieutenant in the Army—he was forward, assured, handsome (*ca va sans dire*) he told me he wanted to be known as the greatest American writer of his generation. And at that time he'd only written a handful of short stories for magazines. But he was seriously working on *Paradise* at the time. Well, of course he *did become* the greatest writer of his generation.

HENRY

And I'm sure he knew many writers of his time.

ZELDA

All our friends were writers of some sort and talent. Writers and their wives and mistresses. And he was generous with his praise for other writers. Most of them were heavy drinkers. Well, we all were, it was the times, the times. Weeks of drinking, sleeping it off, drinking again. I can't remember if we ever ate. And if we did it was delicatessen food—nobody cooked. Edmund Wilson was a close and lasting friend—well, he edited Scott's last, unfinished novel, *The Last Tycoon*, just after Scott's death in '40.

RUMINATING.

Oh dear, has it only been eight years? Seems so much longer. We hadn't met for almost two years before he died. Too young, too young. Too poor, too alone. Too forgotten. Out of print. Somber, beautiful man. But! Optimistic about his working novel. He never saw it published and it was not a success when it finally was.

BACK TO HER STORY.

Ring Lardner was another drinking buddy with an avocation as a writer. George Nathan, Mencken. Dos Passos was a great pal to both of us. Why, Dos came to visit me just the other day in Montgomery. He's been a loyal friend. Not many of them come these days. I would have thought Hemingway would or could have made his way to Mama's house. We were never close but he and Scott were—that is when Hem was not criticizing him for something or other. We often saw Dorothy Parker, Tallulah Bankhead, Don Ogden Stewart—so long ago, two wars ago.

Scott was invited to the Round Table at the Algonquin one or two times. He wasn't as quick witted as Mrs. Parker or Mr. Benchley but he always came home with a few good stories. He later heard of a remark made about him and attributed to one member of the Round Table. It was reported that Edna Ferber had listed F. Scott Fitzgerald as one of America's ten dullest writers. He *loved* telling that story.

Well, there is another story that was making the rounds of every smart party in Manhattan. You may not know this, Mr. Piper, but Edna Ferber is not a beauty, not then, not now. In fact she is quite homely—ugly, some would say. There came a time when Noel Coward was a guest of the Algonquin regulars. At one point, possibly after the soup course he, Noel, looked at Edna and exclaimed, "Why, Edna, you look almost like a man!" To which she replied, "So do you." Scott loved writers. *We* loved writers. Then of course after we decided to move to Paris we found the expatriates, more Americans than Parisians, surely. And then there was Ernest.

HENRY

Hemingway.

ZELDA

Is there another?

For some reason, I never understood just why they became so very close, Hem and Scott. And we women were inevitably excluded from the cabal they created. When I say 'excluded' I mean we were ignored. Hadley and I seemed just along for the drunken ride.

I never liked Hemingway, thought he was bogus as a writer and as a real man, an artifice he prodigiously put forward. Scott was impressed and sought out his favor. Interesting, at the time Scott had published a best-selling novel, Hemingway nothing except some short stories. Of course all that changed in the end. Scott's dead. Today Ernest's considered the laureate of American literature. Isn't it strange about nature, Mr. Piper?

HENRY

Nature. In what way, Miz Sayer?

ZELDA

In every way, Mr. Piper. Indeed, we're all nature's creatures. Now that does not exclude the existence of God as the creator of man, not at all, the argument supports it. But the quirkiness of nature, predictable though it may be, is a conundrum, don't you agree?

In what way you may ask. Well, speaking of death for instance: nature by its very nature is a continuum. One would think, that is people would think, that nature would in some way celebrate the life and death of men or a specific man (I do not exclude women here), some profound indication that *a life had been led.*

HENRY

A BIT CONFUSED

Yes.

ZELDA

Yes, well, I'm glad you're with me here. But when one searches for some indication, sign—some salutation that a life has passed over, nature simply moves on and on forever leaving no sign. I walk five miles a day. And I see the same landscape, the flora, the streams, the mountains. It seems to me that nature could express a *passing* with some subtle bow to that creature who no longer exists on this earth. For instance a slight diversion of the creek; a hill top shaved imperceptibly; a swale where lupine bloom where they had never bloomed before.

Well, that is a question that has puzzled me since last Thursday.

Are you comfortable, Mr. Piper? Would you like a glass of water?

HENRY

No thank you, I'm fine, just fine.

CHANGE OF SUBJECT

Ah, you spent a good deal of time in Europe in the 20's, in Paris I think.

ZELDA

Actually we spent some time in Paris and it wasn't always good.

Well, I shouldn't say that, Paris was exciting, gorgeous. And Scott was finishing up *Gatsby,* so not all was a loss. How we managed I'll never know. Even with the unbelievable rate of exchange we were still broke. Neither Scott nor I ever managed the money we had. Better to have put it all into Scottie's three-year-old hands, for surely she would have been a better bookkeeper than her ridiculous parents. We did not leave our drinking habits behind, the only difference in France was that we drank out of crystal instead of glass—but, by golly we drank. Scott went through long periods of twenty-four-hour binges—I did my share.

Scribner's wanted the corrected proofs of *Gatsby* and for weeks the only response his editor got from Scott was a plea for yet another advance.

But it did happen: *The Great Gatsby.* Three years in the writing and finally, in 1925, it exploded on the scene. But the reviews were mostly negative to bad. Even so it sold about 20,000 copies. Today, of course, it is hailed a classic. We thought we were rich with the $6,500 check Scribner's sent. It was going and gone in a week. By this time we were both writers but we could never learn to spell the word *discipline.*

I am not a practical person, Mr. Piper, I just want the people in charge to make sure that there's enough money in the bank to cover the rent. I know poverty. Well, that isn't true, not at all. I was poor but I never *knew* I was poor. We just kept spending on extravagant bobbles, liquor, fur coats, mammoth automobiles, posh hotel suites—all for pleasure and, well frankly, to show off.

Now, I know it isn't fashionable these days to talk about a certain political persuasion. But I have given the idea of *Fascism* some thought lately. It's more of a philosophy than a political movement, that is, it is to me. What it suggests is *order, discipline*—there's that word again. Can order and discipline be bad things for a society? I think not. If the word *Fascism* offends, then we must call it something else. And I'm currently thinking of just that these last few days. I want you to consider doing the same, Mr. Piper. You're a journalist and you have a voice to the public. If you'd like I could write a piece for your editorial page and who knows, it could be syndicated all over the country. I wouldn't ask for a byline, I'm no longer in the public eye.

HENRY

AFTER ANOTHER AWKWARD PAUSE

You mentioned writing. I think you have written some short fiction yourself, Miz Sayer.

ZELDA

Short fiction? Yes, *short fiction*, a term that I sincerely hope has gone out of fashion. It has always seemed to me to be a dismissive, even a pejorative term. Writing is writing. Two thousand words may be no less valuable than twenty thousand.

Need I remind you that F Scott Fitzgerald began his career writing *short stories* for magazines—to rave reviews and remarkable public acceptance. And yes, I too published many—many *successful* stories for years. As I look back now, I can't help but feel somehow used, yes, that's the word, used. In fact there's no denying that even at the time when we were both writing I felt exploited by my own husband.

HENRY

Oh?

ZELDA

Strong words I suppose. At the time I didn't comment on what was happening. I was so happy to be productive, to be doing something, don't you know. I had published under my married name several articles on the decline and fall of the Flapper—that was for the popular magazine, *College Humor*. Readers loved those pieces and I loved the attention.

After that I worked very hard on a collection of short stories which Scott insisted on editing. Of course, I was thrilled that he thought what I had done was worth his time and talent. All went well. We went to Scribner's who agreed to publish it. As it turned out *Flappers and Philosophers*, a collection of my short stories, was published under the name of *F. Scott Fitzgerald*. The hurt was devastating. Instead of protesting his appropriation of my modest talent I drank and he drank and we fought over who would pick up his ironed shirts at the laundry.

Looking back to my girlhood—well, when I was a sophomore in high school I loved to write—I wrote all the time. My family never encouraged my writing talents such as they were. I exasperated my father; my very *being* drove him to distraction. I recall at one Sunday night dinner, announcing that I had become a poet. My mother was delighted, my father less so.

PICKS UP POEM FROM DESK

Now, Mr. Piper, I apparently kept this poem and just last week Scottie found it in some of my Montgomery papers. I remember distinctly reading this poem at the table, really to defy my father's harsh assessment of me. Well, I can tell you it did the trick. It is a poem that defines just who his least favorite daughter was. I wonder if you'd care to hear it? It's quite dear and accomplished for a girl of sixteen. It's all about me.

SHE READS

PEOPLE WILL TALK AND PEOPLE WILL SAY
THAT I AM FAR TOO LIGHT AND GAY
I MUST ADMIT THAT I'VE MADE A HIT
BUT IN SPITE OF MY WHIRL
I'M A SENSIBLE GIRL
PEOPLE WILL TALK OF A POOR DEBUTANTE
THEY'LL SAY I DON'T KNOW WHAT I WANT
I'M COMING OUT BUT WITHOUT A DOUBT

IN SPITE OF MY WHIRL
I'M A SENSIBLE GIRL
SURE I'M FOND OF ECCENTRICITY
SURE I LIKE SMALL PUBLICITY
BUT I DON'T CARE FOR ORCHIDS AND PEARLS
LIKE SOME OF THOSE SILLY GLAMOUR GIRLS
PEOPLE HAVE TALKED AND PEOPLE HAVE SAID
THAT I HAVE HARDLY A THOUGHT IN MY HEAD
NOW I'M NOT POOR BUT I'M NOT A BORE
IN SPITE OF MY WHIRL, I'M A SENSIBLE GIRL

Well, you see it *is* all about me. But you know that was true for both of us, Scott and me. Almost everything we wrote was about ourselves. We must have been the most narcissistic American writers in history! *(LAUGHS)* We were, we were.

And we haven't for a moment talked about my novel. You of course know that I published *Save Me the Waltz* in '32. It is very good even though it's been out of print for some time. Have you read it? Well, you must. Once again it's all about us, Scott and Zelda. *(LAUGHS)* Scott was furious when he read it. "But, Goofo, it's only fiction," I pleaded. Of course we both knew it was pure biography. I'm very proud of that book. It was popular with many readers. In fact one man thought so much about it he wrote a song called *Save Me the Waltz*. I'll sing it for you later.

Now, Mr. Piper, what surprises me is that you've not

asked why I am living in this hospital. Are you merely being polite—well, you certainly are a polite young man—or are you ... not interested?

HENRY

To be honest, Miz Sayer, I didn't want to pry. But you said earlier that you live at your family home in Montgomery when not here at Highland.

ZELDA

You're very kind, Mr. Piper. The fact is I've been in and out of *these places* for years, from France to Switzerland; from New York to Asheville. I have lived a kind of hell for as long as I can remember. Oh, not today, not all the time. I find pleasures in life.

When Scott was alive I begged him to let me go home to Montgomery and Mama. He listened to the doctors, and there were legions of them, and didn't for a moment listen to me. Surely Scott meant well. I kept pleading with him that he was spending so much money we didn't have to keep me in chains—yes, hyperbole but at times that's what I actually think. That is when I can think at all. *(AWKWARD LAUGHTER)* Why on earth am I telling you these things! Because, well there is madness here. I have told the psychiatrists, the dietitians, the phrenologists, the neurologists, I have told them all that it is *these places* that make one mad. *(SHE STANDS ABRUPTLY)* I am mad.

THERE IS A SUSTAINED PAUSE. ZELDA MOVES GRACEFULLY ABOUT THE ROOM. SHE IS DANCING.

ZELDA

Where were we? So many times these last years I seem to lose my concentration. Concentration. Have I offered you lunch? Oh, of course you're here to talk about F. Scott Fitzgerald.

I have always wanted to dance. Did you know at one time I was offered a season with the Naples Opera, as lead danseur in the corps de ballet? Yes, you no doubt do. Everybody knew.

Dancing was both the happiest and least happy time of my life. I danced as a child, I'm speaking of the classical dance, ballet. Many years later, this was in Paris, I decided that a dancing career was what I wanted. I was in my mid-twenties and many thought I was too old for a career. I refused to believe any of them. I studied under Madame Lubov Egorova the ballet teacher of the Ballets Russe of Diaghilev. That was my goal, to dance for Diaghilev. Madame and I became very close, I worshipped her. She encouraged me, nurtured me. *(RUSSIAN ACCENTED) "But Cherie, you must practice, practice. The grand theatres are longing for your entrance. Selda Sayernova will captivate and overwhelm the Ballet Russe!"* I practiced five, six hours a day. Madame was with me for a year. Scott hated what I was doing and did everything he could to discourage me. Finally he got to

Madame and they agreed I would never be the dancer of my passion. I was beaten. It was another blow to my ego. It took me many years to forgive Scott. I wonder if I really have. And so for the first time I asked myself, who am I?

The wife of a great American writer? Yes. But who am *I* ?

And then, and then the world seemed to fall apart for me.

Mr. Piper, now that we've had our lunch this might be a good time to pray. Would you kneel with me? God will look kindly on us for taking time to acknowledge his presence.

THEY KNEEL

He is everywhere, including this terrible place. He is joyful each time I return home to Mama. To be honest, I think He's just slumming when He's here.

SHE RETURNS TO HER CHAIR

That's quite enough, Mr. Piper.

EMBARRASSED HE RETURNS TO HIS CHAIR

I often think of the Murphys, Sara and Gerald. Do you know them? They were responsible for all of our delicious days on the French Riviera, Antibes. Sara was the perfect hostess and best chum and Gerald was charming, talented and the inspiration for Scott's character Dick Diver in *Tender is the Night*. They built a house there. Well, it was a villa, in fact they named it Villa America. We were guests there so often! Well, there were times when Gerald asked us to leave for misbehaving.

Lord, one night Scott destroyed an entire collection of antique Hungarian crystal glasses—he tossed them over the ramparts onto the rocks below. Irreplaceable. Well, even if they were we couldn't have begun to afford even the tissue paper to wrap them.

We were always broke and the Murphys knew that. *(LAUGHS)* So did everyone. And now you do, Mr. Piper.

But everyone came to Villa America. We met Cole Porter, Somerset Maugham and one of his boyfriends; Dos Passos was always around and so was Carl Vechten, Philip Barry, Ed Wilson, even Picasso—my goodness listen to me, name dropper. The Sheilah Graham of the South of France! Hemingway and Scott were often seen on the terrace talking books and emptying their glasses. But I spent the days on the beach. I tanned and swam and sipped wine with crushed ice all day long. I was going through some old trunks at mama's the other day and came across a familiar and beautiful wool bathing suit. It smelled of the sun on the beach at Antibes. The experience was more than nostalgia, it was *beauty recalled*. Dear Sara provided marvelous picnics and Gerald painted and was amused by the lot of us.

Mr. Piper, speaking of my novel, you know, I mentioned it earlier, *Save Me the Waltz*? I set many scenes of that story on the beach at Antibes. Now the book is fiction, you understand. But in reality it's closer to real happenings than any fiction. In my book the lead female character meets and falls in love with a handsome French aviator. To be honest it's my story. Yes, it is. His name was Jozen and I fell in love with him. In *Waltz* my character has an affair with him. In life, well, so did I. Scott guessed although I never admitted to him. He was hurt and furious and even threatened to lock me in our house to keep me from my aviator. And if you think he was upset about the real Jozen he blew sky high when he read the proofs of my novel. The episode changed our relationship—it was never the same. Drink helped us get through the worst of it.

Are you a writer, Mr. Piper? Well, of course you are, you write about culture for the papers. What I mean to ask is do you have ambition to publish? fiction? the novel?

HENRY

I've been putting in some time, when I have time, into writing a fictional adventure story of the Civil War. Nothing much to show for it.

ZELDA

Ambition, that's what it amounts to, ambition. I was ambitious from as early as I can remember. I wanted to do everything when I was young and, as time would tell, until this very day. I wanted to dance and I did; to write and I did; to paint—well that canvas will support what I mean. My focus would change over the years. And after many years in and out of *these places* and with little or no emotional and spiritual support from Scott or my family I've returned to my love of the written word.

HENRY

You're writing again. Will it be a follow-up to *Save Me the Waltz* after all these years? Could be interesting.

ZELDA

What an absolutely wonderful idea, Mr. Piper. I must remember that. Well, just look at this mountain of foolscap. I'm certainly in the game. But today my interests are entirely directed to the Holy Bible. I read the gospels, embrace the messages therein, and create my own epistles for modern times. It is God who speaks to me as I write; I feel His presence, his direction. I no longer own a Bible.

Did I tell you of Scott's funeral?

HENRY

No, I don't think so.

ZELDA

I was unable to attend. Scottie forbade me so I stayed in Montgomery with Mama. I wanted to at least write the eulogy but even that dignity was denied me. The solitude of a lunatic is never broken, we endure.

Scott was a Catholic but was denied burial in consecrated ground by the Baltimore bishop due to the fact that his books were on the "proscribed" list. *Proscribed*, that was his word. Now, I was told this much later and I'll never forget it: A Protestant minister officiated and he was heard saying, "The only reason I agreed to give this service was to get the body in the ground. He was a no-good drunken bum, and the world was well rid of him."

That for one of the English speaking world's greatest writers.

I wonder if you would like to go for a swim?

HENRY

Oh, I … I'm fine. I'm not really a swimmer.

ZELDA

Well, you surprise me, Mr. Piper, you were never out of the water at Antibes. I can't recall, did you stay with the Murphys or with Ernest and Hadley? You remember, we were at Juan Les Pines in a cozy little villa. But that was last year. Time Marches On. *(LAUGHS)*

HENRY

Did your husband spend a great deal of time in Hollywood? I know *The Great Gatsby* was filmed as a silent movie in the 20s. Were you with him?

ZELDA

We both went out to Hollywood. Beautiful and glamourous. The movie stars were all gorgeous, both women and men. And the parties were every night. Scott was a celebrity then. We rented a house with a swimming pool. Scottie's nanny came with us. Scott was assigned a movie while waiting for *Gatsby* to finish. He hated the work and most of all the people. Except a little bit of a thing, a mere girl, an actress, Lois Moran. He denied it but I know he had an affair with her. I was furious, but then I had a short memory, there *was* a certain French aviator in my résumé.

The movie was released and it was terrible by everyone's standard. We couldn't get out of town fast enough.

HENRY

That was in the 20s. I know that Scott died in California before the war.

ZELDA

Scott is there even as we speak, Mr. Piper. At least I think he is. He sends copious letters from somewhere out west. I have come to the conclusion he's a spy for Mr. Truman. There is a war coming, with Russia this time around, one can count on it. Scott's really too well recognized to be a successful spy. I just hope he won't change his good looks with a facelift. Well, President Truman won't let him down.

He's also making movies. And he has a novel on his desk. Something to do with secrets and plotting and guns—very contemporary. I know too that he's seeing a woman as part of his work for the government. She's posing as a gossip columnist but she's most assuredly a spy, also. This modern world is complicated, don't you agree?

Will you take lunch with me, Mr. Piper?

HENRY

Oh, no thank you, Miz Sayer. It's getting on six o'clock. I've had my lunch.

ZELDA

You have changed a great deal. Never lived by the clock. We neither of us do. Is it Hollywood that has done this, the movie stars and grand parties. Why have you stayed away for so long?

Have I been bad. Goofo, the solitude of a lunatic is never broken. I've told you time after time, love me when I least deserve it and when I most need it.

HENRY IS MADE NERVOUS BY THIS FANTASY BUT IS CAREFUL NOT TO SHOW IT

I love you even if there isn't any me or any love, or even any life. I love you. Come to me. Be with me. We were always perfect partners. Without you my dearest dearest I could not see or feel or think—or live. I wouldn't want to. I love you so and I'm never in all our lives going to let us be apart another night. Oh, darling Goofo, Where has it all gone, where have we gone? *In the end death is the only elegance.*

SUSTAINED PAUSE

You know, of course, that I paint, Mr. Piper. And I'm not one of those 'Sunday painters' we all know of. I've shown more than one time in Montgomery and, mind you, New York City. Scott was responsible for several shows of my work. (INDICATING EASEL) This is a work in progress. That's a fancy way of saying I don't know what on earth I have in mind. (LAUGHS) I'll show it to you after lunch.

HENRY

Yes, I would like to see your work.

ZELDA

Women must have their own creative lives. I never learned to cook and to clean and to wash. I didn't want to. Let someone else do that and pay them well for the effort. I may have been unrealistic about my dancing, well, that's what I was told over and over again and finally forced to accept the fact that I would never dance for Diaghilev. Didn't for a moment stop me from *creating*. I wrote to minor acclaim, and today I paint with a kind of gusto. But never, never was I accepted for myself—I was always the wife of America's greatest author.

And it is only now when I am imprisoned in this madhouse that I am brave enough to call myself *Zelda Sayer*.

SHE FLINGS HERSELF FROM HER CHAIR/PACES THE ROOM

I want to go home, Scott!

THE PLEA IS NOT TO HENRY BUT TO AN INVISIBLE SCOTT

Why have you listened to the doctors and not to my fragile yet *reasonable* pleas. This place is like a forced castration for me. Enforced inactivity maddens me beyond endurance. Of course I'm crazy, who wouldn't be crazy trapped in this privileged class, tastefully decorated jail cell!

I am loved in Montgomery. I am loved by my mama and my friends who believe in me.

SHE STOPS/PAUSES

Oh, dearest, mount your white horse and come for me. Why is there excitement and comfort and happiness where you are and nowhere else in the world? Damn it, come for me! *I love you.*

SHE RETURNS TO HER CHAIR/CALM AGAIN

All I want is to be very young and very irresponsible and to feel that my life is my own to live and be happy and to die in my own way and to please myself. (LAUGHS) I'm really only myself when I'm somebody else to whom I have endowed with these wonderful qualities from my imagination. There are mornings when I wake and ask myself what person will I be that day. It's a splendid exercise. Yesterday I decided to be Zelda Sayer—now *that* was surely a curious adventure.

Are you a married man, Mr. Piper?

HENRY

No. At least not yet. There is someone.

ZELDA

The war. Didn't we just finish a war? Scott enlisted and was commissioned a second lieutenant, stationed just outside Montgomery. Well, that's where we courted. The war ended before he could be sent to the front. My goodness, he was handsome in his uniform. Miss Sayer was swept off her feet. I, a seventeen year old debutante and a tad naughty at times. I loved to show off. But I didn't care, life was fun and that's what I wanted, fun—always did. A year after Scott proposed we were both living in New York.

HENRY

You must have had a wonderful life.

ZELDA

We did. But nothing could have survived the way we lived. We get something in our life and as soon as we get it, it gets us.

We found our dreams on the infinite promise of American advertising. You know I still believe that one can learn to play the piano by mail and that mud will give you a perfect complexion. This is America after all.

SHE LAUGHS.

HENRY

Did Scott Fitzgerald struggle with his writing? Were you aware of that?

ZELDA

F. Scott Fitzgerald had many struggles, not the least of which was his writing. He was essentially an exhibitionist, at least in his early days. I know something about that and I may have been the tutor in his pursuits. Drink was our downfall and a major reason for his procrastination ultimately, and at times his inability to sit before the typewriter. And yes, he and his friends often blamed me for interrupting his muse. Nonsense. Then, of course, there was the struggle with his enormous ego. Scott was quite serious when he said he expected to become America's greatest writer. His ambition—well, his ambition was not unlike Jay Gatsby's. Read those early chapters. For that matter reread the book and you'll find that all through the novel it is Gatsby showing off. There was a lot of F Scott Fitzgerald in Jay Gatsby. You may not know this but it was I who was responsible for the final title of *The Great Gatsby*. He had flirted with various titles, which didn't seem right at all. And as it turned out I was right—*Gatsby* it was, and is. So you see I am not just a footnote in F Scott Fitzgerald's biography. He was difficult; we were both difficult. Impossible at times—too often times.

HENRY

You say that without any sense of criticism. Do you see that as love? It certainly seems so.

ZELDA

I see it as love, yes. More to the point I see it as indulgence. I suppose he would say the same of me. Even so, memories should be sharp when one has nothing more to live for. I may have lost some of my mind through the brilliance of medical science but I have not forgotten even one midnight cocktail with F Scott Fitzgerald.

Thank God for God. *(LAUGHS)* Without Him the universe would be chaotic, the symmetry unsettled, spiritual life wouldn't exist. Excuse me for being so intellectual. I know, Mr. Piper, you would prefer something nice and feminine and affectionate.

HENRY

Not at all. *(PAUSE)* I did a little research before coming here, Miz Sayer.

ZELDA

I'm sure you did, Mr. Piper. And what did you find other than the tabloids' endless pictorial anecdotes in the Sunday rotogravures?

HENRY

Dorothy Parker ...

ZELDA

Yes, Dotty, never really liked her. Was she witty?

HENRY

Well, let me quote her if I may: "They (that's you and Scott) were riding on the top of a cab down Fifth Avenue. They both looked as though they had just stepped out of the sun. Their youth was striking. Everyone wanted to meet them."

Witty, no. But certainly glorifying, wouldn't you agree?

SHE IGNORES HIM. CHANGES THE SUBJECT

ZELDA

The Beautiful and the Damned. Just as a large portion of the American reading public read it, so did I. Not in proofs but after it was published. As always I took my time with each page so that I could discuss it with Scott. Anyway I was asked to review it for the *Post*—obviously a publicity ploy. It seemed to me that on one page I recognized a portion of an old diary of mine which had mysteriously disappeared shortly after we were married. Well, it wasn't the first time and not the last. Apparently plagiarism begins at home.

The Beautiful and the Damned. Come to think of it, that could be our story only that Scott was the beautiful and I, the damned.

CALLS OFFSTAGE

Charmaine, be sure to keep that door ajar.

It's not getting any cooler in here. There's just this one tiny fan.

This is not the poor people's ward, I'm a paying guest. Charmaine, did you hear me?

CHARMAINE

OFFSTAGE

I'm right here, Miz Sayer. The door's open and as you know it shouldn't be. I know it's plenty hot. Anything you-all want?

ZELDA

Come to think of it, yes there is. How 'bout the master key to the front door of this joint.

CHARMAINE

OFFSTAGE

Now, Miz Zelda, you know I couldn't do anything like that. It's against the rules.

ZELDA

Well then why not a chocolate fudge cake with a file in it.

CHARMAINE

OFFSTAGE

You're raggin' me, Miz Zelda.

ZELDA

I am, Charmaine. But you're a good sport.

HENRY

She *is* a good sport.

ZELDA

I used to be a good sport. Years and years ago. When life was fun and lived for every moment. I expected great things to happen and no doubt that's one of the reasons why they did. I refused to be bored because I wasn't boring. A good sport? I wasn't such a good anything at hospital after hospital where I was stuffed with pills, subjected to electric shock treatments, fed dog food diets and—lo and behold, found insane. My goodness, what a surprise. There's not a vestige left of the Zelda Sayer *I* knew. Look at me, a captive of myself, someone, well someone I don't recognize on *odd* days of the week. *(LAUGHS)* I love a good pun!

AN AWKWARD PAUSE

REFERRING TO THE STACK OF PAPERS ON THE TABLE

I haven't a clue why they call it 'writer's block.'

SHE SWEEPS THE PILE TO THE FLOOR

I never had a block. I published countless stories. Scott was merciless in his criticism, even when he thought they were good—then he stole them. Yes, he did. I knew that he knew that I knew.

Little was said. *(SOBBING)* Oh, God how I love him. Hate him.

HENRY STANDS

Scott! You're not going? You're always going, running away. Stay, I'll make drinks. We'll talk about Princeton, the Pig Lady, Paul Whiteman. Don't go.

HENRY

Miz Sayer, I've overstayed my visit. I thank you for your time.

ZELDA

You're not Scott. You're an imposter. And you've taken advantage of me. Pretending to be F. Scott Fitzgerald when you're not. I knew there was something not right the minute you entered my house. All you wanted was my Bible tracts. And you were going to publish them under your own name. Well, that's not going to happen because I've been in touch with Scribner's and they have signed a contract with me to publish my life's work in two grand volumes.

HENRY

I wish you all the success in the world, Miz Sayer. It has been a pleasure meeting you. I'll look forward to your publication.

ZELDA

CALMED

Why, thank you, Mr. Piper, how very kind. Now, you work hard and one day you may be editing that newspaper of yours. Remember your prayers. And, Mr. Piper, if you should forget now and then to say your prayers, I'll be praying *for* you.

HENRY

Thank you. Goodbye.

HE EXITS

ZELDA SITS FOR A MOMENT, CONTENTED

ZELDA

You out there, Charmaine? Well, of course you are.

CHARMAINE

OFFSTAGE

It's gettin' late, Miz Zelda. My shift's about over. Time to lock up for the night.

ZELDA

It can't be night, we haven't had morning. Oh, I suppose you're right, you always are, Charmaine. Go ahead, lock up the lockup.

Too early to sleep, I'll get back to my painting.

CHARMAINE

OFFSTAGE

Don't stay up too late. You know what the doctors say.

ZELDA

I know what the doctors say, and say and say. But tonight I feel exhilarated, I don't want to sleep. Wasn't it wonderful seeing Scott?

CHARMAINE

OFFSTAGE

Yes, Miz Zelda, it was swell. Goodnight.

WE HEAR THE LOCK CONNECT.

SHE MOVES TO THE EASEL AND REACHES FOR

A BRUSH. SHE BEGINS TO SING "SAVE ME THE WALTZ" AT THE SAME TIME AS THE OFFSTAGE MUSIC WITH VOCAL IS HEARD. SHE PUTS BRUSH TO CANVAS. LIGHTS DIM TO BLACKOUT WITH THE EXCEPTION OF ONE SPOT ON ZELDA'S PROFILE. SHE FREEZES IN TABLEAU.

NEWSCAST:

Mutual News:

Another death was announced this morning, that of 48 year old Mrs. Scott Fitzgerald, widow of the late American novelist F Scott Fitzgerald who died in Hollywood, California in 1940. Mrs. Fitzgerald's charred remains were found in her room following a kitchen fire on the lower floor of an Asheville, North Carolina sanitarium. Investigators noted that the door to her chambers was locked in accordance with the hospital's regulations. Identification was made by the discovery of a dance slipper under the remains.

In the latest movie news the romantic comedy, "The Bride Goes Wild," with Van Johnson and June Allyson, is a box office hit all over the country ...

LIGHTS FADE TO BLACKOUT.

THE CURTAIN FALLS.

Paris is Paris is Paris
Gertrude Stein in Paris

GERTRUDE STEIN (1874-1946) was a self-proclaimed American genius. Although her critics might disagree, she was probably right in that assessment. Born in a small town in Pennsylvania and raised in Oakland and San Francisco, she studied medicine at Johns Hopkins, leaving, without an MD degree, to follow her brother to Paris in the early days of the twentieth century. And Paris is where she discovered life, love, a sense of place—and fame as a writer, poet, and art collector.

The most accomplished and celebrated artists of the day visited her rooms in the rue de Fleurus. She knew "everybody who was everybody" in the arts, music, and theatre. She was a loyal friend to many and an unforgiving foe to those she felt had betrayed her. Perhaps her most significant relationship, other than her life partner, Alice B. Toklas, was with Pablo Picasso.

In the following play, we find Miss Stein working at her parlor table. Looking up from her page, she is delighted to discover she has company. She has time and she loves nothing better than talking. She loves to talk—particularly about herself. The year is 1946.

PARIS IS PARIS IS PARIS
GERTRUDE STEIN IN PARIS

HOUSE LIGHTS DIM TO HALF. MUSIC: RAVEL CONCERTO. HOUSE LIGHTS OUT. CURTAIN RISES TO REVEAL A LARGE WOMAN SITTING IN A REGAL CHAIR, CENTER STAGE. SHE IS WRITING AT A TABLE TO HER IMMEDIATE RIGHT. SHE IS CONCENTRATING ON HER WORK. NOTE: CHARACTER REMAINS SEATED THROUGHOUT THE PLAY.

OFFSTAGE ANNOUNCEMENT

This is Paris. The year is 1945. The woman sitting before us is Gertrude Stein. She is a writer, a critic, a poet. This is her apartment in the rue Christine where she and her companion, Alice B. Toklas, live. Tonight Miss Stein has agreed to talk to us. She has some thoughts she would like to share.

MUSIC CONTINUES FOR ANOTHER 20 SECONDS AND FADES. STEIN STOPS HER WRITING, READS IT OVER BRIEFLY AND SETS IT ASIDE. SHE LOOKS UP, SHADES HER EYES FROM THE LIGHT AND PERUSES THE AUDIENCE. SHE PICKS UP THE WRITING TABLET. REFERRING TO IT SHE SAYS ...

GERTRUDE STEIN

This is brilliant. Brilliant, I always know it will be brilliant because it *is* brilliant. I never rewrite, I never edit. I know it will be right because I write and I know it will be right. I'll put it aside for Miss Toklas' typewriter. She types, Miss Toklas. I write. She types.

You should know Miss Toklas is out marketing for our food. She has been out most of the day for cheese. Cheese to please is not easily found these days in Paris, France. Cheese that is. Since the Occupation food is still scarce. Scarcely any cheese. The cheese we like.

Through the years Miss Toklas has been entirely in charge of the kitchen. She is a wonderful cook and she cooks many dishes we like, and that is why she cooks because that is what we like. Miss Toklas was known especially for her omelettes, which she would prepare for our friends. For those of whom we were less fond, she would fry an egg. Matisse comes to mind. Her pies are sought after, so after a lovely dinner we eat her pies. She bakes bread and makes chili, so American. We're often out for lunch after having just tea and bread with butter for breakfast. I am often a late sleeper. Miss Toklas is not and so she prepares a Spartan breakfast for me when I wake. It is an excellent routine and it pleases me. Miss Toklas says it pleases her as well. Excellent.

I like everything about America. My boys, the soldiers, bring us food from America. I like everything about America but not its cheese. The soldiers like American cheese, like pliable orange wax. I like butter and so do the soldiers but I don't like peanut butter but I like the soldiers. But if these are the only criticisms I have about America then I have no criticism. Except of course about cheese. And peanut butter. There is better butter than peanut butter, better in Paris, France, better butter and better cheese. Well, I suppose one could call me a butter and cheese man! *(A HEARTY LAUGH)*

To begin is more interesting than to finish.

Now I know you have heard my casual statement when referring to Oakland, California. "There is no there there." The fact is there *is* no there there. However you should know that I was not born in Oakland, California as many believe. I was born in a small burg just out of Pittsburg, West Allegany, the Oakland of Pennsylvania. As good fortune would have it, we moved to San Francisco at the end of the last century. So long ago. I like San Francisco. I had a grand family life. Mother dead. Father dead. I didn't finish high school. I didn't need to. I needed to move on to study. As a young person I had many interests—what to study? Radcliffe and Harvard, then I decided on medicine at Johns Hopkins, Baltimore.

I decided to move from medicine to ... well, you should know I wanted to be historical. Where can one become historical? I decided to move to where then? To Paris, France where one could become historical. The year is 1904. So long ago.

My beloved brother, Leo Stein, and I shared an apartment at Number 27, rue de Fleurus. Brother was early on interested in painting and the getting of art. We collaborated with what money we had, we collaborated in buying art. At the time I was writing. I was writing every day and night, I was writing night and day. Leo painted. I wrote. He talked. I was silent.

A person needs removal. One must take time to close the tablet and look to the outside world. Leo and I, along with some newfound friends explored the South of France and Italy. Lovely, but closer to Paris and rue de Fleurus is where I wanted to be. And the ideal to idle in Luxembourg. The gardens. The walks, the strolling, the fountains, the museum. After tea and a bun I could return to my tablet refreshed. Refreshed I was. Refreshed, rejuvenated and refueled. I was writing, working, writing on my first work, a superb collection of stories, *Three Lives*. Leo painted; I wrote. He talked; I was silent.

SHE LOOKS OFFSTAGE, LEFT

Miss Toklas?

Miss Toklas. A taskmaster. She does everything. I like that. That she does everything, Miss Toklas. I like to be cared for. I have always been cared for. I think it is a good thing. I like it.

Brother, ever searching for the getting of art, discovered a small gallery where hung two paintings. He wanted them. And we took them with just enough francs to make the payment. You should know that these were a Picasso and a Cezanne. The beginning of the collection. A collection of nice pictures. Of course many more were added over the early years, the years in Paris, France. Oh, so many nice pictures: Gauguin, Matisse, Manet, Renoir, Daumier, Braque. Photos of Man Ray—he photographed everyone who was everyone in Paris, everyone.

I have tried over the years to recall the severing of my ties with brother Leo. What I do recall is that he looked at me one unhappy day and said he was smart and I was stupid. That remark alone certainly contributed to the rift. In fact that rift gave a lift to my swift drift. (Oh, how I love the sound, the tenor of words!) *(LAUGHS)* Now I was obliged to make a life of my own. I don't remember a final, shattering, cleavage but there must have been one, or was it that we both went silently into the night. Right. The collection was split and I was left with the Picassos. To be *left* with Picassos is nothing to grieve over. Grieve indeed. My new and much admired friend, Pablo Picasso, was often at my tea table.

He was a presence, a manly man, a witty companion and a genius. Speaking of genius, Miss Toklas says there are only two geniuses in the world: Pablo Picasso and Gertrude Stein. And I agree with her. And I have the proof of the matter. Picasso's portrait of Gertrude Stein, 1906. When he first showed it to me I was startled. "But, Picasso, it doesn't look like me." "It will, Gertrude, it will," he said.

I've mentioned Miss Toklas. Well, Miss Toklas has been mentioned, she's here but not here because Miss Toklas is out at the markets as I've mentioned. We, Miss Toklas and I, met in 1907, that being her first visit to Paris where I was living and am still living with Miss Toklas. I had just published *Three Lives* to the considerable interest of American readers. Yes, we began to form a a close relationship due to mutual interests and passions for the arts, but mostly due to Miss Toklas' interest in Gertrude Stein. I can appreciate that, it's quite natural. And then in, I think it was, it was just after the New Year that we began to share number 27—1910 I think it was. Miss Toklas will know.

So now I had a new love and a secretary to aid me in my daunting new passion, the finishing of *The Making of Americans* which I published the following year. Have you read it? Miss Toklas thinks it's brilliant. Miss Toklas is seldom wrong.

It would be wrong to say that my new companion is simply a secretary. She is a handmaiden, a confidant, a partner in crime in the making of art. And *The Making of Americans*. Speaking of books, one could say Miss Toklas and Miss Stein are on the same page. *(LAUGHS)*

I cannot deny the hurt I felt when Leo ran off with some of our most beautiful pictures. He ran with all the Renoirs and most hurting with Cezanne's "Apples." "The Apples," "the Apples," Cezanne's "Apples." Picasso felt my hurt and so promised to paint me another apple. And he did paint another apple. For me. At the same time I was able to buy my first Juan Gris. I speak of these pictures as though they were mere bibelots, trinkets. Not so, that is it is not so that I think so. Great moments of the moderne, "the new" were happening. Not only in the visual arts but on the page as well. Well, I'll give you an example. In London I published *Tender Buttons*, the very first of my cubist writings. Obscure to some, those some with no perceptible imagination. Listen. Listen, I say. It's not the words but the sounds and the rhythms of those words and phrases. Listen. Listen as Miss Toklas listens. She listens. You see I had invented a new form, a specific language mixture of inner monologues, dialogues, poetic plays if you will. When you read Gertrude Stein you must clear your mind and listen, listen. Are you listening? *(PAUSE)*

Now the Great War is upon us. It's 1917. Miss Toklas was a bit overcome when I invited her to the street one afternoon. Not for lunch, mind you, but to view our newest art acquisition, "Auntie," a handsome Ford automobile, a van. Together we journeyed south to Nimes to lend our collective hand to the aid of the American Front and French war wounded. And where we met American Doughboys for the first time. And we were smitten. And we were charmed and we were touched. Miss Toklas insisted we adopt some of those young men and we did. And we heard from them for many years after the armistice. After the cease-fire we drove to Alsace to distribute food and clothing to the civilian population. So devastated, so needy. Our reward? Although we were certainly not looking for one—from the French government, the *Medaille de la Reconnaissance Francaise.* Auntie took us back to Paris.

It was this hotel keeper who said what it is said I said that the war generation was the lost generation. Well, yes, I said that. And yet it was a time, beginning in 1920, when there was a thrust, a blast of new and raw talent in the arts. To begin with Sylvia Beach opened her bookstore in the Latin Quarter. Everybody who was everybody, including Miss Toklas and myself gave, Shakespeare and Company our custom. Not only a bookstore but a meeting place. And the Americans came, they came because they had to come and that's why they came.

Over the many years I've lived in Paris I've met many artists. When I say artists I mean those who make art in any form. I have always, since I can remember, I've always been a writer, but that doesn't mean that that was my only interest. As I've mentioned, my brother and I supported the painters and now I have what I and many consider a valued collection which covers the walls in this apartment. But as to the writers, those who write and are writers, many have been and are my friends. Some came to me off the boulevards and others I met through Sylvia Beach. One who visited us often was a kind and gentle soul and a giant of a writer. Well, he was a writer but not a giant even though he managed to break at least one chair every time he visited. What to do with Ezra Pound? Well, it took Miss Toklas to devise a solution. She would offer him a solid wooden bench each time he walked into the room. We never heard a complaint.

Paul Bowles was a favorite. He was such a young man when we met him. So determined to write. Curiously, he was very caught up with religion, especially eastern religions. He was like a son to us and loved being in our company. Just a boy. He will be read in the future. He's read now.

I much admired Thornton Wilder. He was a friend and visited from America often. There came the time when he had stopped off in Paris after having spent time in Vienna with Freud. We were of course all ears to hear of the experience, Wilder's experience. In that respect he was silent. He spoke of the old man with reverence. I would never be a candidate for psychoanalysis. I understand it is all based on sexual fantasies. That is for men. Women do not have sexual fantasies. Still I do wonder what Wilder told Freud. Or for that matter what Freud told Wilder.

I had an opportunity to meet with T.S. Eliot. I had ventured to ask if he would publish one of my short pieces in his magazine, *The Criterion.* Eliot sat uncomfortably in a rather comfortable chair clutching his umbrella. He simply would not give it up. Instead of an answer to my query he asked his own question: "Who," he asked, "was your authority for consistent use of the split infinitive?" In the end he did publish me. Gossip came over the Channel that Eliot had remarked that Gertrude Stein was not for *The Criterion.* I was rather pleased by the compliment. We did not meet again.

As to painters, I knew many of them. I love the so called Cubist movement and that's why I acquired three paintings of Juan Gris, my favorite being *Roses*, a Cubist collage. Gris was from Spain. We met when he was twenty-seven and just married to Josette. Still he was a womanizer. He loved to dance and was often at the many dancehalls in Paris. He was effusive and intellectual and awed by another landsman, Picasso, whom he addressed as cher maître, much to Picasso's annoyance. He was a good and loyal friend even though he was temperamental and downright impossible at times. Impossible is not so bad.

Sylvia Beach introduced so many of the Americans. I recall the first time I met both Sherwood Anderson and Ernest Hemingway, both of whom I, we, took to. Miss Toklas was less sure of Hemingway but that was later. It is no secret that Sylvia believed in James Joyce. She was intent on our meeting, Joyce and I. Probably not a good idea. Joyce was pompous and untalented, and Beach was, in my opinion foolish to have published him.

We met only the one time and as Miss Toklas opined, "one time was too many."

This was around the time when we opened number 27 to our new friends for Saturday evening salons. Everyone was welcome until they were not welcome which happened from time to time which was a welcome idea. Everybody who was everybody visited. I'm forever grateful to Miss Toklas for entertaining the wives and/or the mistresses of the hearty, talented, egocentric, brilliant men who were making art and history in the Paris of those remarkable years. We talked about everything. I preferred to talk books, language, even syntax, which of course I have never believed in. At the same time Miss Toklas was attending to the women: Hadley, Zelda, Margaret, Josette, Olga, et al. It was all very chummy.

I saw very little of Fitzgerald and that was not unhappy making since he was a liquorite. The quintessential American man was Fitzgerald. The boy next door, I suppose. Demons haunted that boy next door. Sherwood Anderson was a frequent visitor and we collaborated now and then. A good, kind man who published the great novels set in the American heartland.

But it was Hemingway who most wanted to impress. Young, raw, semi-talented, he was driven to write. He never arrived without a handful of papers. What did I think of this or that or this idea or that fiction, this or that. He sought my approval which I am reluctant to give to any writer save myself. There was one evening when he burst into number 27 clutching one dog-eared, limp piece of foolscap. He was obviously pleased with what he had written. I was less pleased with what I read. Like a child waiting for his Pablum he beseeched my good-news appraisal. Honesty is what is important to me, honesty in all things. Our eyes met. There was a pause. And then I said, honestly, "Hemingway, a paragraph does not literature make." I could be wrong, but at that moment, I think I heard a titter from Miss Toklas in the kitchen. Even so, I know he loved me, well, I thought he loved me and I became a kind of mentor or traffic cop for this brash, hardy, handsome bull of a manly man with not a little talent yet unequal to his ego. "Hemingway," I said, "you want to be a writer, you must read, read, read other writers. Read Henry James, he is the master.

And what good fortune for Miss Toklas and Miss Stein for we became godmothers to Hemingway's first son, John, known as 'Bumby.' We loved babies, all babies. And many of our friends brought their little ones for visits. And sometimes we would kidnap these little ones and take them to Luxembourg for an outing. And so the birth of Bumby was a happy occasion. Hemingway and I remained good friends for many years until, until … well, until.

I am often quoted and rightly so. I should like to clarify the famous *rose* conundrum that is so often spoken in concert with my name, Gertrude Stein. I have self-published many books, some with great success, others with less. Success. In '22 there was *Geography and Plays,* a collection of poems and prose, forwarded by Sherwood Anderson. In that volume there is an early poem, *Sacred Emily.* I had written a line, "Rose is rose is a rose is a rose." A year later in another collection, *An Elucidation,* the phrase became and is still quoted as "a rose is a rose is a rose." There is a difference. One must look for it.

The twenties were remarkable in terms of artistic energy and achievement. My world was of course the written word but of equal interest and passion was art—the pictures. Picasso and I spent a goodly amount of time together. We were best friends. We spoke the same language when, of course, we didn't speak the same language but we spoke the same language anyway. And this is the same time that the American composer, Virgil Thompson walked into number 27. And so I added yet another passion to my repertoire, music. And I was to write several operas with Thompson. Not bad for someone with a tin ear. *(LAUGHS)*

I really shouldn't say that. I like music of all kinds. Ravel was an acquaintance, Debussy also. I must admit I had a favorite song that I sang at a moment's notice upon requests, although there were not many requests and never at a moment's notice. You see, there was an American novel of the Old West published just after the turn of the century. In 1916 it was made into a moving picture and became very popular. At the same time a song based upon that story was written and appeared on the music stands of most parlors in America. The book and the song have the same title, *The Trail of the Lonesome Pine*. And to this day it is my favorite song. If Miss Toklas were here just now she would set a key for me with her mouth organ. She is not here just now.

Now, I wonder where she can be, Miss Toklas? Well, the larder must be tended to if not filled, and she is exacting in her provisioning. She is a bargaining expert. One has to be, she tells me, always. Always she tells me but especially at this time in this year at the end of the war.

We had been spoiled in the South where we grew our own food and even traded with our neighbors—eggplant for eggs, sweet peas for sugar. We entertained the American G.I.S. Those lovely boys would bring us special treats of chocolate and coffee and oh so many things deprived of during the war. I'm certain she'll be here soon. I've asked her to use what taxis are available but she insists on the Metro. She's still a hardy woman and she's adorable. I hope you can meet her. I wonder what's taking her so long?

A house in the country is not the same as a country house. In our case we had both in one. Our love for the country was never more satisfied than our sweet petite maison south of Paris. We rented this retreat for many years. I have a lovely poem about that house and perhaps all houses, not just that house which was our house.

SHE READS

The house was just twinkling in the moonlight
And inside it, twinkling in delight
Is my baby bright
Twinkling with delight in the house twinkling
With the moonlight
Bless my baby, bless my baby bright
Bless my baby twinkling with delight
In the house twinkling in the moonlight
Her hubby dear likes to cheer when he thinks
And he always thinks when he knows and he always
Knows that his blessed baby wifey is all here and he
Is all hers, and sticks to her like burrs, blessed baby

Many friends visited there in our country house and life went on a pace not unlike that in Paris. Picasso was often in residence as was Virgil Thompson, Hemingway, Janet Flanner and her companion. Solito Solano, Balmain, Sherwood Anderson.

Jane Heap, the editor of *The Little Review*, was often with us. Always curious, well, she was after all a writer and publisher. One day she asked for an interview. I'm always reluctant to do that in that that is what I am reluctant to do.

And so it was a game of sorts. I've kept a copy of that time.

SHE SEARCHES HER LARGE SCRAPBOOK

Ha, here it is, the original, there not being any copies. Looking at it afresh I find it honest, for that is what I always am, and witty. Wit can be honest just as honesty can be witty. The two are not mutually exclusive nor should they be. Jane Heap asks...(SHE READS)

What would you most like to do, to know, to be?

My answer: "But I am."

Why wouldn't you change places with any other human being?

"Because I am I."

What do you look forward to?

"More of the same."

What has been the happiest moment of your life?

"My birthday."

What do you like most about yourself?

"Almost anything."

What things do you really like?

"What I like."

What is your world view?

"I like to look at it."

Why do you go on living?

"I am."

(LAUGHS)

Now, that's enough of that.

One of the reasons for this lovely book I have here before me is that it contains so many photographs. Years and years of photographs, mostly by Man Ray. And later after we met him in London, Cecil Beaton, An elegant photographer of taste and theatricality. We became very fond of Man Ray, Miss Toklas and I. Our story is here in these pages. If you could see what I see you will see that Miss Toklas is not a smiler. I am a smiler in most of these photographs. Except when I am asked for a portrait then I do not smile, somewhat glum, chum. *(LAUGHS)*

It was our Ford cars that took us to the country. We loved Fords and we had several over the years. We loved Fords and dogs, and we had several of those—dogs. We loved Fords and dogs equally. Our dogs appear in many of these photos and so do our Fords, together, dogs and Fords. One day Mr. Ford, or one of his minions, came to us petitioning us to appear in an advertisement for Ford, not Mr. Ford, but the Ford car. And there we were in a magazine of the time with a lovely Ford car, an open Ford car, one without a top except for the rain. Miss Toklas sits in the back seat and I stand at the passenger door with one leg extended not unlike a ballerina. Ah, if only Diaghilev could have seen me. Nijinsky would have had cause to worry. And that is another reason why we liked our Fords because we were photographed before one and we were paid money to stand in front of Mr. Ford's Ford.

SHE SINGS (after a fashion)

"In the blue ridge mountains of Virginia, by the trail of the lonesome pine..."

Yes, this is my favorite song, an American song and I love it, it is my favorite song. And I love America and Americans. America is my native land. That I live here in Paris is clear to me for it is not America, it is Paris. I am at home here but it is not America. I am at work here because I work here. I visit America. Miss Toklas and I visited America in 1934 and we saw much of America which we love. We stood at the Grand Canyon feeling much like standing at the top of the Empire State building.

We were invited everywhere by everybody who was everybody. I was invited to speak to many young American students from east to west, meaning both coasts, one on the east and one on the west, both with water but not the same water.

My new opera, *Four Saints in Three Acts*, had reached Broadway and there was my name in electric lights, very exciting. Virgil Thompson and I saw our work performed wonderfully. We were hosted about that noisy, dirty, surreal, magnificent metropolis by all the artists and writers and musicians who made art. As busy and excited as I was, I was even at that time working on another opera. I'm calling it *The Mother of Us All* and again Thompson will write the music, I, the libretto. All very productive and exciting.

We visited San Francisco where both Miss Toklas and I had lived many years in our youth. And we trained to Los Angeles and Hollywood. Hollywood, it was *swell*, as they say in Hollywood. Miss Toklas liked it and so we both liked it. And we met Dashiell Hammett and Anita Loos and King Vidor who was directing everything in moving pictures. And we met Charlie Chaplin, a gentle person. We talked and talked. We both liked talking but each one had to stop to be polite and let the other one say something. *(LAUGHS)*

When I was at a dinner party in Beverly Hills, near Hollywood, there were a great number of stars of the cinema. After the dinner all these people were sitting there in front of me and I did not know what it was all about or what they wanted, and finally one blurted out, "What we want to know is how do you get so much publicity?" So I told them, "By having such a small audience. Begin with a small audience. If that small audience really believes, they make a big noise. And a big audience does not make a big noise at all." I don't know that I answered their question.

We trained north again, this time to Monterey, California. We stopped at a grand hotel, the Del Monte Hotel, very nice as were the people there in Monterey. They knew who I was which was no surprise since they were a small audience but making a big noise.

Our American experience was very satisfying. We saw so much of the land and the people and the tall buildings and the not-so-tall buildings, like the Indian tents, not like East Indians, but American Indians, redskins. They danced for us and smoked and chanted and painted their faces with colors. And we both came away with our scalps. *(LAUGHS)*

We were invited to the University of California, in Berkeley where I spoke. There were mostly young women in the audience. Miss Toklas thought men were afraid of me. I don't know why, I'm not afraid of them. Well, the afternoon went very well, we were served tea and buns and then there were questions from the young women.

I was most interested in the questions relating to grammar and, of all things, punctuation. Miss Toklas took a remark from a pretty girl as a kind of challenge. There has never been and never will be a time when I am not up on my feet for a challenge. She, the young lady, had apparently read my monograph, *Poetry and Grammar,* where I discuss the use of the comma. She seemed to disagree with the text. Let me quote myself here. As I did for the lost young lady.

READING

"A comma does nothing but make easy a thing that if you like it enough is easy enough without the comma. A long complicated sentence would force itself upon you, make you know yourself knowing it and the comma. Well, at the most the comma is a poor period that it lets you stop and take a breath but if you want to take a breath you ought to know yourself that you want to take a breath. It is not like stopping altogether which is what a period does. Stopping altogether has something to do with going on. But taking a breath, well you are always taking a breath and why emphasize one breath rather than another breath. Anyway that is the way I felt about it very very strongly. And so I almost never use a comma. The longer more complicated sentence the greater the number of the same kinds of words I had following one after another, the more the very many more I had of them the more I felt the passionate need of their taking care of themselves by

themselves and not helping them, and thereby enfeebling them by putting in a comma."

So, you see, it is quite simple. And the young lady who asked the question was now put right.

Americans are optimistic unlike the French and Europeans. And yet Americans know what it is like to have disillusion. It is a contradiction, disillusion and optimism. But it is American. I am an American. America is my country and Paris is my home town. I love America. I love my home town.

It always did bother me that the American public was more interested in me than in my work. After all, there is no sense in it because if it were not for my work they would not be interested in me so why should they not be interested in my work more than in me? That is one of the things one has to worry about in America.

Well, it was a wonderful experience, this journey to my country.

In every city, town and burg we visited, reporters would ask for interviews. Miss Toklas was not happy to be followed around by people carrying tablets and pencils but I rather enjoyed the experience. I like to talk. Their questions were very often the same from city to city: Do you have a new book? Why do you live in Paris instead of New York or Albuquerque? What does this or that poem mean?

Just before boarding the ship that would take me back to my home town I answered one reporter's question this way: Yes, I am married. I mean I am married to America, it is so beautiful. And I am coming back to America sometime, someday not too long. I never knew it was so beautiful. It was like a bachelor who goes along fine for twenty-five years and then decides to get married. That is the way I feel, I mean about America.

Opening the door to number 27 was a wonderful feeling. Home again. That that wonderful feeling was fleeting was the cause of disappointment in reading an article in the magazine *Transition,* a collaborative effort by some of those who were welcomed many a Saturday at my salons. The title of the article? *Testimony Against Gertrude Stein.* It was an attack on my writing, especially *The Autobiography of Alice B. Toklas.*

And it was signed by Matisse, Braque and others who should have known better. Well, I knew better. I began a lecture tour through France and then to London and Oxford. I was never once asked to explain myself. The fact that I was there was explanation enough. I liked them and they liked me. I did not see Matisse again. I did see Braque one time as I did Marie Laurencin but never again. As the British say, a storm in a teacup. But really, just a drizzle.

The sharing of a life is not something that comes easily. There will always be those times when a careless word, a wrong interpretation, a dustup will interfere with the smooth workings of a shared life. A disagreement over some issue, trivial though it may be, must never be left on the back burner. An intellectual argument is not so serious as a personal one. Miss Toklas and Miss Stein have found an excellent exercise to ward off such potential personal hurt. We write letters. We write letters to each other. We express our feelings openly and succinctly. These letters or notes may go on in a correspondence for several days. At the end, in a meeting over tea, peace is declared—unconditional surrender on both our parts. I have a note here from Miss Toklas and I will read it to you since she is not here because she would not like to hear it I think.

Dear Miss Stein, It seems I must clarify the meaning as to my negative feelings for Ernest Hemingway. He has for many years been a friend to both of us. We have jointly enjoyed his visits, intensive though they have tended to be.

It is only in the last year or so that I have come to realize his ego is perhaps too large for this modest-sized apartment. He dominates whenever he comes. He is bombastic. He speaks only to you while the others present are ignored.

You are and have been his greatest supporter and defender from when he first walked through our door. I think he has taken advantage of your good counsel, your sweet nature, and your good will.

It is not that I dislike him, I am more and more uncomfortable around him.

I know this may be a disappointment to you and I regret that. My concern is for Gertrude Stein. I hope you will understand my point of view. I hope too that we can put an end to this really very slight difference of opinion. May I invite you to take tea with me at number 27 rue de Fleurus on Thursday at four? Yours, Alice B. Toklas.

I have here my answer to Miss Toklas.

My Dear Miss Toklas, I take both sugar and milk in my tea. Signed, Gertrude Stein.

Well, isn't that an excellent way to move beyond disagreement?

You'll want to hear this poem, it's from my *Portraits and Prayers.*

If you hear her snore

It is not before you love her

You love her so that to be her beau is

Very lovely

She is sweetly there and her curly hair

Is very lovely

She is sweetly here and I am very near

And that is very lovely

She is my tender sweet and her little

Feet are stretched out well which is a

Treat and that is very lovely

There is something about a person who is American and who speaks English and who lives in France but does not speak French even though that person does speak French but not in France because that person speaks English in France. That is I. And I cannot tell you why. I write in English and I think in English and I dream in English. But I live in France. I live in Paris, France.

But now there is a war to change all that. Miss Stein receives a warning from the American Consulate to leave Paris, to leave France. It is 1939. But what I can see is that Paris is peaceful and exciting. A good friend, an American, suggests we, Miss Toklas and I, return to lecture in the United States. He tempts us to go to Hollywood where there is interest in a film of *The Autobiography of Alice B. Toklas*. Everyone who is everyone has yet another idea for our departure from France. We see no facts to suggest our leaving. But then the Occupation comes and we move to our house in the country where we have friends. And where I become very productive with three novels: *Ida, Mrs. Reynolds,* and *The Winner Loses: A Picture of Occupied France.*

I was a sympathizer with Marshal Petain's politics of the Armistice. At the same time another friend intervenes with the Vichy regime in order to secure our protection—we are Americans. And we are Jews. Our skills were of great help in these four years. Miss Toklas's cooking and my black market dealing were nothing short of professional.

It was a strange time. Feeding ourselves was not an easy proposition. We planted a vegetable garden and traded carrots for flour. We acquired a goat and named her Bizette and we walked and walked to find food. At one point Pierre Balmain came to the country to design warm clothing for us made out of scraps of fabric, tres chic.

And we had other visitors. In the summer a German officer and some of his staff came to live with us. They just moved in; they were not invited. Not invited.

We were quite fond of them, especially when they portioned some of their rations for us. When the Germans left the Italian troops arrived. The wine was wonderful.

The Maquis were about in those war years. I began to believe in their cause. They were *reds*, of course, but they were patriots of France. Politics, politics. We were all about surviving. And I kept to my writing and I don't know how I found the time but I did.

Wars I Have Seen, and in 1944, *In Savoy: A Play of the Resistance in France.* Both to be published in America.

And then it all ended, the war. Miss Toklas and I greeted the American "G.I.s" in the country. They came and they came and we were ecstatic and so were they. They shared everything they had with us and we with them. We mothered them, sang to them and kept them up all hours to talk, talk about their victories, their losses. And their families back home in America. They knew who I was and wanted to know what I was writing currently. My goodness, they even asked me to read some of my poetry.

They wanted to know how we managed to escape the Germans. And we learned the Gestapo had been in our apartment in Paris to look at everything. Naturally I began to have what you might call a delayed fear. I was quite frightened for the first time during the Occupation. Of course, when the Germans were here we were so busy trying to live through each day so it was just once in awhile that we realized we were being watched. But now the Americans were here to tell us of the terrible things that had happened to so many others. So many others. We were shocked along with the rest of the world.

Glory Hallelujah, the news came over the radio that Paris was free. I can't tell you how excited we all were. We were so tired but could not sleep. We ate and drank and kissed everybody. Miss Toklas too. We kissed the boys from Denver and Baltimore and Lincoln—from Detroit and Chicago and Hollywood.

And then the time came for our return to Paris. We were then living at rue Christine, having been routed by a stingy landlord from Number 27. We walked into the apartment to find most of the art still on the walls. The Bosh had been there and had thrown some slight bits and pieces about but the collection was intact. The barbarians mocked us and they threatened to cut the Picassos to shreds only to be stopped by the Paris police and ordered out onto the street.

The days of celebration seemed never to end. I was invited everywhere. Even to step into a "chow line" set up in a fancy Paris hotel. The food was good, good chow. I like good chow now. *(LAUGHS)*.

The "G.I.s" kept pinup girls all over the walls of their barracks like religious icons. They idealized women but when they walked the streets of Paris many of them would be drunk and would leer and insult every woman they met. The American boys were mostly virgins for only virgins would act that way. The spoils of war?

In the months following the victory I had adventures. I flew in a transport over Berlin, I was feted by diplomats, I was celebrated as a great American writer. Which I am. These were heady times for Miss Toklas and Miss Stein.

We had survived the war and thrived in the peace. Such as it was.

LOOKING OFF, RIGHT
CHECKING HER WATCH

Really, she'll be tired tonight after a long shopping day. Well, we'll have a late tea and a light late supper. It's this past war. Food is still so very scarce and Miss Toklas is so particular and demanding with the trade. No one would dare deny her or trick her, not Miss Toklas.

I've not been feeling my best in these last months. Same complaints, same doctors complaining that I complain which of course I do because I complain. My writing has suffered. I have so many ideas for a new poetry volume. It will not be "moderne," it will not be "new," but something entirely original, although I have always been original. I'm calling it *Post War Avant.* I'll get to it soon. I have time. If things do not take long it makes life too short.

I must tell you and though I don't often sound like it I've got plenty of sense. There ain't any answer, there ain't going to be any answer, there never has been any answer—that's the answer.

Ah, but what is the question?

SOUND: A KEY IN A LOCK; THE OPENING OF A DOOR, STAGE RIGHT

Oh, at last, she's home. I want you to meet her. Pussycat, is that you? I'm here by the fire. Come in, come in, where have you been all day? Come in, Pussycat, come in and meet these nice people.

SHE TURNS TO HER RIGHT. HER HAND REACHES OUT IN A GREETING GESTURE. SHE FREEZES IN TABLEAU.

OFFSTAGE ANNOUNCEMENT

Gertrude Stein died at the age of 72 on July 27th, 1946. She is buried in the Paris Cemetery Pere Lachaise.

On her tombstone Gertrude Stein's birthplace is misspelled and the date of her death is confused with that of her brother, Leo.

Alice B. Toklas lived in poverty until her death at 89 in 1967. She is buried next to her companion.

MUSIC W/LYRICS: "ON THE TRAIL OF THE LONESOME PINE"

LIGHTS SLOWLY FADE TO BLACK.

CURTAIN

ACKNOWLEDGEMENTS

Heartflet thanks to Peggy Michael for her encouragement and handholding.

Appreciation to Kyle Ferdinand for his cover design. Thanks too to Margaret Mayer, Richard Flower, and publisher, Patricia Hamilton.

And a bow to two accomplished actors who have brought these ladies to life on the stage: Carol Daly and Rosemary Luke.

TOM PARKS

The author is a playwright and essayist. He spent twenty-five years working as a behind-the-camera professional in the entertainment business before settling in the small California village of Carmel-by-the-Sea. He has written, produced and directed many plays, musicals and dramas on the California Coast. He lives today in a small, forested cottage with his best friend, Mr. Toby, a six year old Maltese.

www.ingramcontent.com/pod-product-compliance
Lightning Source LLC
Chambersburg PA
CBHW031252210726
48287CB00003B/997
* 9 7 8 1 9 3 5 5 3 0 5 6 5 *